Scrap Savers' Stitchery Book

BY SANDRA LOUNSBURY FOOSE

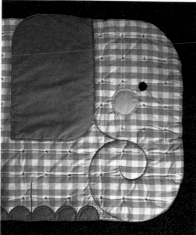

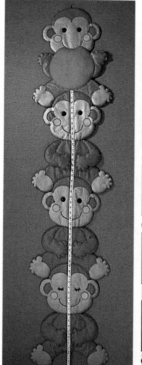

COUNTRYSIDE PRESS
a division of Farm Journal, Inc.
Philadelphia, Pennsylvania

Distributed to the trade by
DOUBLEDAY & COMPANY, INC.,
Garden City, New York

Grateful acknowledgement is made for permission to reprint the following:

Reindeer and Sleigh, reproduced by permission from the December, 1973 issue of *Good House-keeping* magazine.
ⓒ 1973 by The Hearst Corporation.

Washcloth Puppets, reproduced by permission from the October, 1975 issue of *Redbook* magazine.
ⓒ 1975 by The Redbook Publishing Company.

House Banner previously appeared in the May 3, 1977 issue of *Woman's Day.*
ⓒ 1977 by CBS Publications, Inc.

Christmas Ornaments previously appeared in the Winter, 1977 issue of *Good Ideas for Decorating.*

Barn Bag and Animals previously appeared in the January, 1978 issue of *Redbook* magazine.

Book Design: Maureen Sweeney

Photos: Rachel Martens; except pages 38, 54, 71, 105, by author
Pattern Art: by author

ISBN: 0-385-13437-1
Library of Congress Catalog Card Number 77-83595

CONTENTS

SEWING WITH SCRAPS

All of us who sew have a drawer or box or basket somewhere, stuffed with scraps too big or too precious to throw away. And if you're like me, you also have a few ''buys'' neatly folded away—yardage you picked up on sale, irresistible remnants.

The idea behind this book is to use up your store of scraps. To inspire you, here are more than fifty designs and patterns for stuffed toys, pillows, placemats, wall hangings and other gift and household items—including a number of Christmas decorations and tree ornaments. You'll find the makings for many happy gifts in your scrapbag.

If you have fabrics similar to those I've used, and you like the way the design looks—fine. But don't go out and buy new fabrics to match my choices. Your purple cow will be just as delightful as my pink one. When you put your own colors and prints together, you put something of yourself into the design. That's what gives the old patchwork quilts their special charm. They were made from scraps at hand by women who had the courage to do what pleased them. Besides, I fear you might lose your enthusiasm for sewing if you spend too much time shopping for the materials; and I know you'll spend too much money.

Some of my directions do specify scraps by color. But that's mainly for identification—to make it easier for you to relate directions to the color photographs.

Patterns for all the designs are here; as many as possible are drawn full-size, ready for you to trace. Directions explain how to make each item. If there's anything you don't quite understand, look in the How-to Section in the back of the book for more detailed information on cutting patterns, choosing fabrics, sewing, stuffing, attaching appliques and embroidering.

Anyone who manages to finish a book—especially a first book—does so with help. I want to send my thanks in four directions: To my parents, Howard and Sophie Lounsbury, who lovingly provided the opportunities and encouragement for me to develop my design interests. To my editor, Kathy Larson, who turned all my ''scraps'' into a book. To my dear husband, Dean, for saying ''You can do it,'' and for putting up with a lot of dust and quickie dinners. And to my infant daughter—thank you, Tracy, for providing incentive by coming along when you did! Because of you, I was able to make a book and a baby at the same time.

With Tracy now picking curiously at some of my stitchery, I'm struck by the generations who've been somehow involved. It was my two dear grannies, Annie and Maggie, who taught me to sew and I want to dedicate my Scrap Book to their memory.

Sandy Foose

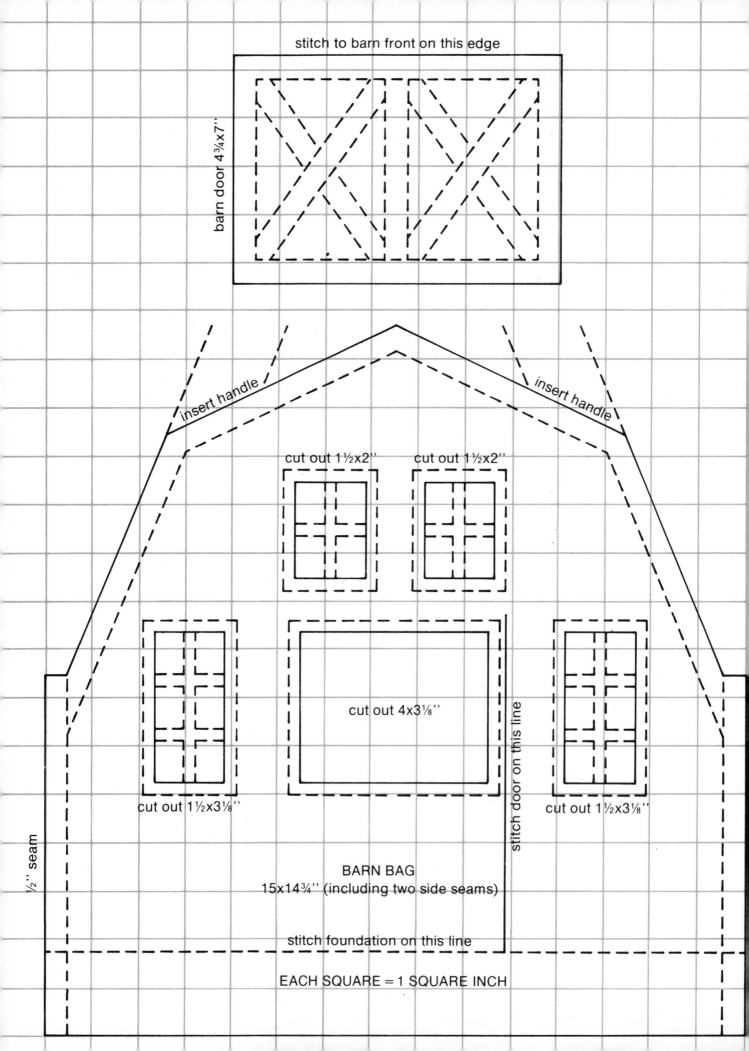

stitch to barn front on this edge

barn door 4¾x7''

insert handle

insert handle

cut out 1½x2''

cut out 1½x2''

cut out 4x3⅛''

stitch door on this line

cut out 1½x3⅛''

cut out 1½x3⅛''

½'' seam

BARN BAG
15x14¾'' (including two side seams)

stitch foundation on this line

EACH SQUARE = 1 SQUARE INCH

As a child plays with the animal toys in this basic barnyard, he may have ideas about who's missing and who should be added! But there's plenty of room inside the barn bag for duplicates of these animals or for some of your own design.

Do choose a sturdy fabric for the bag. I like corduroy because the ribs look like barn boards. After cutting out the windows of the barn (so the animals can peek through), cover raw edges with window frames of white bias tape. Add strips of bias tape, folded, stitched and tacked in place, to make window panes. There's an opening cut out behind the door, too, where the animals go in or out. The door buttons shut after all the animals are safe inside.

This might be a good travel toy to make for your youngster, since no one would have to carry it—you just pick it up and wear it!

BARN BAG

MATERIALS

½ yard heavy red fabric (corduroy, duck or quilted cotton)
½ yard dark fabric (patterned or plain for lining)
Checked fabric, 5x15''
White bias tape, wide, 25'';
   single-fold, 3 yards
Black bias tape, wide, 50''
White jumbo rickrack, 25''
Black ball button, ½''

DIRECTIONS

1. The barn bag is 14x14½''. The pattern—drawn on a ½'' grid—is half the actual size. To enlarge pattern, draw 1'' squares on paper and copy lines from small squares to corresponding large squares, using the squares as a drawing guide. Cut out pattern, and cut out window and door areas on solid lines.

2. Fold red fabric; place bottom of barn pattern along fold. Trace outline of barn; trace window and door areas on barn front. Mark the foundation lines on both front and back. Cut out barn bag, but do not cut out windows or door yet.

3. Using same pattern, cut out lining for barn bag.

4. Pin and baste lining to barn bag, wrong sides together.

5. From check fabric, cut foundation 5x15''. Turn under ½'' on both long edges and press. Fold foundation lengthwise and baste to bottom fold of bag. Then topstitch edges of barn foundation to back and front of barn—allow ease while doing this.

6. Reinforce windows and door opening by machine stitching ⅛'' outside pencil lines. Cut away negative areas on pencil lines.

7. Bind raw edges of window and door openings with white (single-fold) bias tape; machine stitch, catching both sides and mitering the corners.

8. To make window pane muntins, fold a 25'' length of white single-fold bias tape to make a strip ¼'' wide; stitch along both edges. Cut into lengths as follows: six strips, 2''; two strips, 2½''; two strips, 3¾''. Sew in place by hand on lining side of bag.

9. Cut barn door from red fabric 4¾'' wide, 7'' high. Trim with white (single-fold) bias tape, using it flat—½'' wide. Follow pattern design to baste crisscross bars in place; machine stitch.

10. Cut lining for barn door; pin fabrics wrong sides together and bind door edges all around with wide white bias tape.

11. Pin door to barn and machine stitch along right side. Sew button and loop on left side.

12. On front of bag, fold wide black bias tape over edge of roof peak and baste in place, inserting white rickrack trim under edge of tape on front. Also cover roof edge on back of bag with black tape and baste in place.

13. Fold bag, right sides together, and stitch side seams. Trim seams in layers, trim corners and turn right side out.

14. Cut red fabric for strap 4'' wide, 27'' long. Fold strap, right sides together, and stitch along seam; trim seam in layers, turn, press and topstitch length of strap on both sides.

15. Insert strap between front and back at roof line, following slant of roof to get correct angle. Pin roof edges together precisely and baste. Topstitch along roof edges, securing strap, rickrack and tape with this stitching.

stuffed animals

DIRECTIONS

Patterns for animals are actual size. The outline for animal bodies is the *stitching* line. The outline for felt horns, hooves, wings, etc., is the *cutting* line.

1. Trace patterns on tracing paper or sandpaper and cut them out carefully.

2. Lay patterns on wrong side of fabric. With a sharp, soft pencil, trace around pattern directly on fabric. Do not cut fabric before stitching—it's easier to stitch first, then cut out these small animals.

3. Pin two layers of fabric, right sides together and stitch on pencil outlines, using small machine stitches. Each pattern tells where to leave an opening for turning and stuffing.

4. Cut out animal bodies ⅛'' from stitching line. Clip curves and V-angles; trim corners.

5. Turn right side out and stuff lightly. Animals should be soft and rather flat. Close openings neatly with invisible hand stitches, inserting felt pieces as directed.

EMBROIDERY may be done whenever you wish: on the flat single layer of fabric, or after stitched animal is turned and stuffed. See the How-to Section for directions for transferring embroidery outline to fabric and for embroidery stitches.

Use two strands embroidery thread for all embroidery. In addition to embroidering features, I like to edge all the felt pieces with small blanket stitches.

FELT TRIMS are sometimes specified as *double thickness.* Use rubber cement or fusible web to bond two layers of felt together.

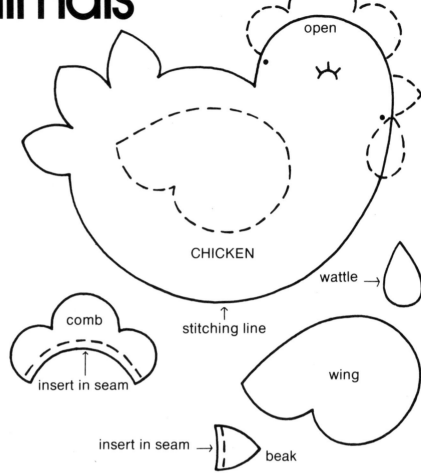

CHICKEN

wattle →

stitching line

comb

insert in seam

wing

insert in seam → beak

ACTUAL SIZE

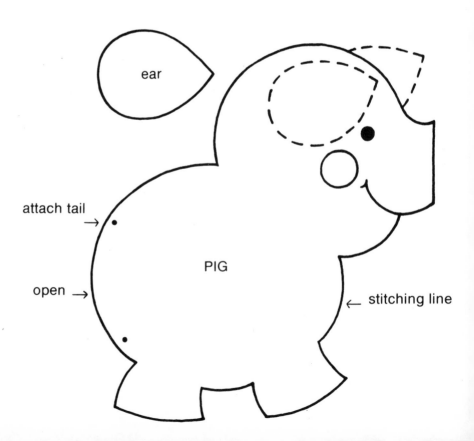

ear

attach tail →

PIG

open →

← stitching line

chicken

MATERIALS

Yellow print scrap, 4x9"
Red felt, 3x3"
Yellow felt, 4x4"
Red, yellow and black embroidery
    thread
Polyester stuffing

DIRECTIONS

1. Trace pattern on yellow print; stitch, cut out and embroider chicken following general directions for stuffed animals. Leave head seam open for turning. Stuff lightly.

2. From red felt, cut two wattles (single thickness) and one comb (double thickness). From yellow felt, cut two wings and one beak (both double thickness). Edge all felt pieces with blanket stitches.

3. Insert comb and beak into open head seam and close seam by hand.

4. Join the two wattles together at front edge and attach to each side of chicken at back edge.

5. Embroider eyes with black thread.

6. Slip-stitch wings to chicken at top edge only so they flap.

pig

MATERIALS

Orange print scrap, 4½x8½"
Orange felt, 3x3"
Orange, pink and black embroidery
    thread
Narrow pink ribbon, 12"
Polyester stuffing

DIRECTIONS

1. Trace pattern on orange print; stitch, cut out and embroider pig following general directions for stuffed animals. Leave opening in back seam for turning. Stuff lightly.

2. Fold felt and bond the two layers together with rubber cement or fusible web. Cut tail ¼x2"; cut two ears.

3. Edge tail with blanket stitches, form a loop and insert both ends into back seam opening. Close seam by hand.

4. Edge ears with blanket stitches and slip-stitch to each side of head, leaving pointed ends free.

5. On both sides of head, embroider pink satin stitch for cheeks, pink outline stitch for mouth and black satin stitch for eyes.

6. Tie ribbon around pig's neck.

horse

MATERIALS

Red, white and blue print scrap,
    7x12"
Red felt, 2x2"
Blue, black, red and pink
    embroidery thread
Polyester stuffing

DIRECTIONS

1. Trace pattern on print scrap; stitch, cut out and embroider horse following general directions for stuffed animals. Leave opening in back seam for turning. Stuff lightly. Close opening by hand.

2. On both sides of head, embroider pink satin stitch for cheeks and nose, black satin stitch for eyes and red outline stitch for mouth.

3. To make tail, thread needle with six strands of blue embroidery thread. Pass needle through fabric at tail dot seven times; cut thread each time leaving fourteen tail pieces about 2" long. Tie these pieces together with one knot. Trim tail threads same length.

attach mane →

attach tail →

open

← stitching line

HORSE

hoof

ACTUAL SIZE

4. To make mane, thread needle with six strands of blue embroidery thread. Pass needle through fabric in mane area (between dots); cut thread and knot. Stitches should be close together. When you get to ears, knot mane threads first on the "back" of one of the ears, then on the "back" of the second ear, so mane appears to go between ears. Trim mane threads to about ½".

5. From red felt, cut four hooves; applique to front and back of each leg with blanket stitches.

COW

MATERIALS

Pink and green print scrap, 6x12"
White felt, 4x4"
Green felt, 2x3"
Black, pink, green and white
  embroidery thread
Polyester stuffing

DIRECTIONS

1. Trace pattern on print scrap; stitch, cut out and embroider cow following general directions for stuffed animals. Leave seam open at top of head for turning. Clip carefully into V-shaped area below the ears to avoid puckering. Turn and stuff lightly. Close opening by hand.

2. From white felt, cut one nose piece and two tail tufts (both single thickness) and one head tuft (double thickness). From green felt, cut two hooves (single thickness) and one horn piece (double thickness).

3. Applique nose piece to cow's head with blanket stitches. Just before finishing, push a little extra stuffing under nose piece so nose will be puffy.

4. Edge horn piece and head tuft with blanket stitches. Lay horn piece on head, cover with tuft and stitch to head.

5. Sandwich end of tail between felt tail tuft pieces and edge tuft with blanket stitches all around.

6. Applique hoof pieces to feet with blanket stitches.

7. Embroider black satin stitch for eyes, pink satin stitch for nose and pink outline stitch for mouth.

open

tail tuft

nose

horns

COW

hoof

ACTUAL SIZE

stitching line

head tuft

mouse

MATERIALS

Green and white print scrap,
 4½x10''
Light pink felt, 3x3''
Light pink, black, white and green
 embroidery thread
Narrow white ribbon, 8''

DIRECTIONS

1. Trace pattern on green print
scrap; stitch, cut out and embroider
mouse following general directions
for stuffed animals. Leave opening
in base seam for turning. Stuff
lightly. Close opening by hand.

2. Stitch through ears with running stitches to make them bend.

3. From pink felt, cut two inner
ears (single thickness), and applique to ears using blanket stitches.

4. Embroider pink satin stitch for
nose, black satin stitch for eyes,
black straight stitch (one strand
only) for eyebrows and mouth, white
outline stitch for whiskers.

5. To make tail, thread needle
with six strands of green embroidery
thread. Pass needle through fabric
to the middle of the back three
times; cut thread each time leaving
six tail pieces about 6'' long. Braid
to length of 2¾'' and knot. Clip ends
leaving a tassel about ¾'' long (total
tail length, 3½'').

6. Tie ribbon around neck.

cat

MATERIALS

Turquoise and white print scrap,
 5x10''
Medium pink, black and white
 embroidery thread
Narrow yellow ribbon, 12''
Polyester stuffing

DIRECTIONS

1. Trace pattern on turquoise print
scrap; stitch, cut out and embroider
cat following general directions for

stuffed animals. Leave opening in
base seam for turning. Stuff lightly.
Close opening by hand.

2. Embroider black satin stitch for
eyes, black straight stitch for eyebrows, black outline stitch for
mouth, white outline stitch for whiskers, pink satin stitch for nose and
inner ears.

3. Stitch through ears with running stitches to make them bend.

4. Tie ribbon around neck.

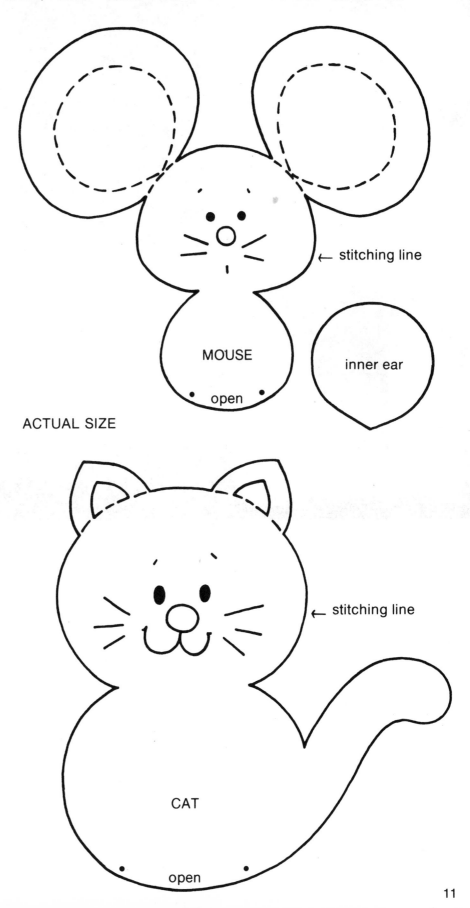

← stitching line

MOUSE

open

inner ear

ACTUAL SIZE

← stitching line

CAT

open

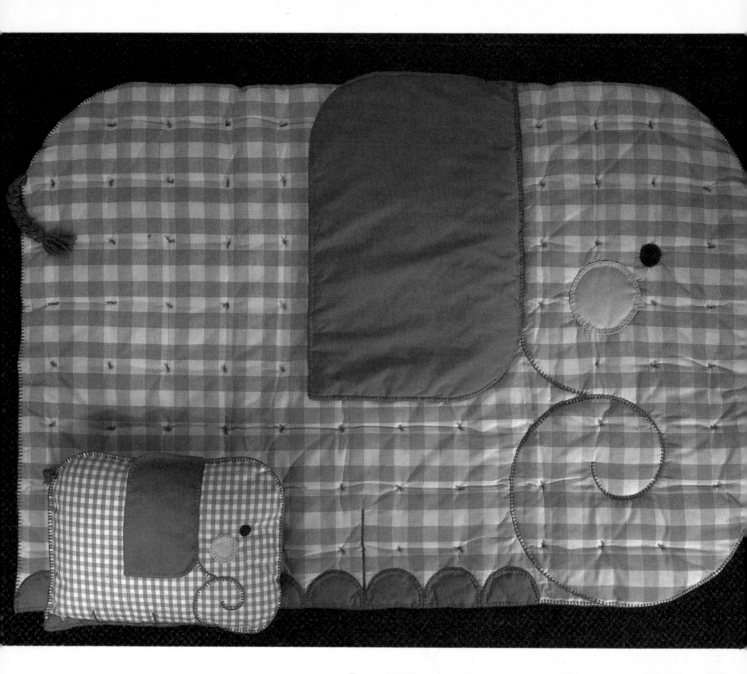

CRIB QUILT
& PILLOW

When I found checked gingham in different sizes at the store, I started thinking about mamas and babies. Wouldn't it be fun to cut a mama elephant quilt from the big inch-size checks and a baby elephant pillow from little quarter-inch checks? As a crib set, such a pair would be a perfect gift for a very special little person. Or either one alone would be most welcome in a nursery.

If you use gingham with 1'' checks, it is possible to enlarge the quilt pattern directly on the fabric simply by counting squares: Each square on the pattern equals one square on the fabric. The finished mama elephant is 51 squares from trunk to tail and 35 squares high.

The ears on both the pillow and the quilt are free and floppy—attached only along one side—which makes them useful for playing peek-a-boo. If you don't want floppy ears, cut the ear front only and applique it in place.

My elephants are aqua blue and white checks with bright green ears, toes and backing. You might like to make red and white elephants with blue ears and toes—or orange and white with bright pink. For a neat-looking quilt, match the yarn for blanket stitching to the color you choose for quilt back and ears.

mama elephant quilt

MATERIALS

1½ yards aqua-checked gingham for quilt top (1'' checks; fabric 45'' wide)

2⅜ yards solid green fabric (45'' wide) for quilt back and trim. (Baby pillow can be cut from scraps.)

Polyester quilt batting, 37x52'' for quilt, 16x23'' for ear. (For an extra-puffy quilt, use two layers in quilt.)

Bright pink scrap, 5½x5½''

Black scrap, 2x2''

Green yarn, 2 ounces (50 grams), 3-ply sport weight

Pink yarn, 6 yards

Black yarn, 2 yards

(All yarn should be washable)

DIRECTIONS

Finished quilt is approximately 35x51''. The pattern is one-fifth actual size; each square in the pattern = 1 square inch.

1. Enlarge the pattern following directions in How-to Section, tracing outline for elephant directly on 1'' checked gingham with a basting thread or very light pencil line. (If you do not use a checked fabric, make pattern on paper marked with 1'' squares.) Enlarge and cut patterns for ear (15x21½''), cheek (4¾''), eye (1⅜''), toes (2½x3¾''). *Pattern line is stitching line.*

(I'm fussy about pencil lines showing, so I usually trace patterns on the wrong side of fabric; then I baste along tracing line to get the pattern outline on the face of fabric. Be sure to flip pattern if you trace on wrong side.)

2. Lay gingham over quilt backing, wrong sides together; pin. Cut out quilt top and backing, adding ½'' seam allowance. Remove pins.

3. On quilt top, mark positions for features: trunk, toes, cheek, ear and eye (see transfer directions in How-to Section).

4. From folded green fabric, cut ear front and back, adding ½'' seam allowance.

5. Use quilt top and ear as patterns to cut batting (batting should have the same ½'' seam allowance). Cut two layers of batting for an extra-puffy quilt. Cut one layer of batting for ear.

6. Working on a large flat surface, layer quilt pieces in this order: batting (both layers); quilt backing (right side up); quilt top (wrong side up). Carefully line up edges and pin. Machine stitch ½'' from edge, leaving 12'' opening at center bottom edge. Remove pins. Trim seams; trim batting very close to seam line; clip curves.

7. Turn quilt right side out, gently pulling out edges. Close bottom opening with hand stitches.

8. Again working on a large flat surface, pin all around outside edge of quilt to position seam line exactly on edge; baste; remove pins. To keep quilt layers from shifting, also pin and baste along (but not on) head and trunk lines.

9. Layer ear pieces in this order: batting; ear back (right side up); ear front (wrong side up). Carefully line up edges and pin. Machine stitch ½'' from edge, leaving 6'' opening. Remove pins. Trim seams; trim batting very close to seam lines; clip curves.

10. Turn ear right side out, gently pulling out edges. Close opening with hand stitches. Pin all around ear to position seam line exactly on edge; baste; remove pins.

11. From green fabric, cut out nine toes, adding ¼'' hem allowance all around each toe. Cut out pink cheek and black eye, adding ¼'' hem allowance. Turn under hem allowance, finger-press and baste. (If you cut curved edges with pinking shears, you'll find it easier to turn under hem allowance.)

12. Now you're ready to attach ear and finish the quilt with applique and embroidery (see How-to Section for stitches). Pin ear in place on quilt front; sew ear to quilt along head line only with invisible hand stitches; remove pins. With green yarn, blanket-stitch ear to quilt along head line, passing needle through to back of quilt to hold ear

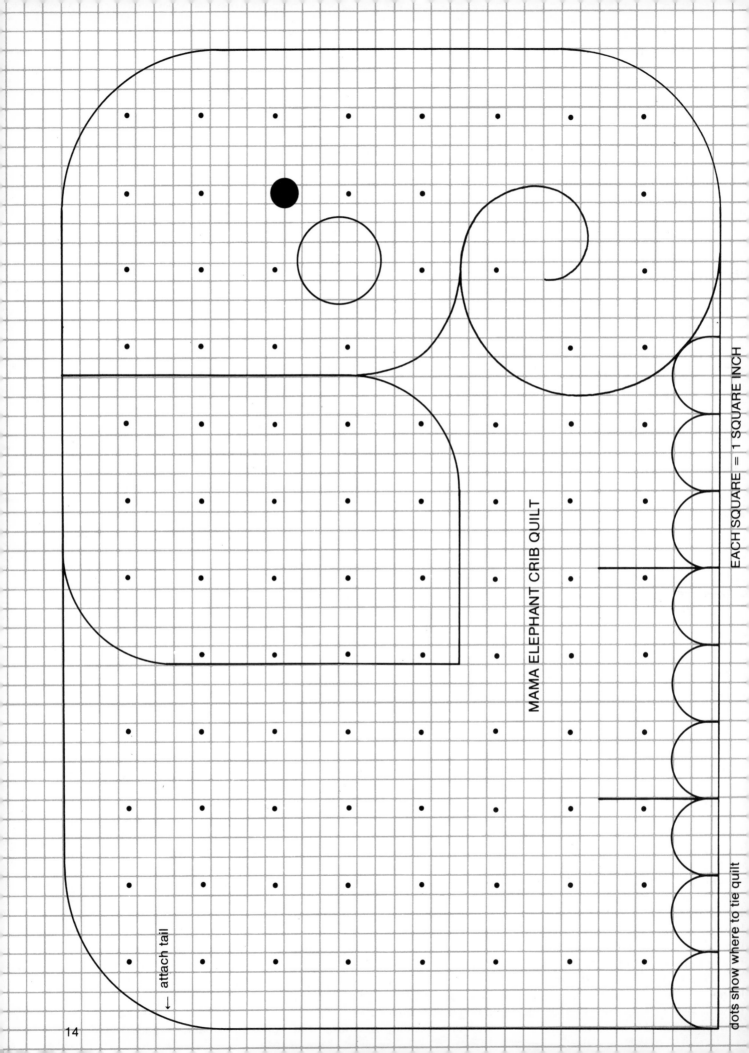

MAMA ELEPHANT CRIB QUILT

EACH SQUARE = 1 SQUARE INCH

dots show where to tie quilt

← attach tail

14

securely; continue blanket stitch to meet trunk line. Finish remaining three edges of ear with blanket stitch, but do not stitch them to quilt.

13. Pin all toes in place along lower edge; sew toes to quilt top with invisible hand stitches; remove pins. With green yarn, blanket-stitch rounded tops of toes to quilt top only; but along bottom edge, blanket-stitch through all layers.

14. Starting at inner circle of trunk, blanket-stitch on trunk line, passing needle through to back of quilt. When you reach quilt edge, continue to embroider blanket stitches all around outside edge of quilt, stitching through all layers. (Be sure to blanket-stitch the edge between toe and trunk.)

15. With green yarn, chain-stitch leg lines, passing needle through to back of quilt.

16. Pin and sew black eye and pink cheek in place, using invisible hand stitches. With matching yarn, blanket-stitch edges, passing needle through to back of quilt.

17. Quilt ties are spaced 4'' apart—in the center of every fourth square on 1'' checked fabric. Dots on pattern show placement. Note that quilt is tied *under* the ear, not through the ear. Use green yarn to make ties. Insert needle through quilt front to back; take a tiny stitch (⅛'' to ¼'') and come back to front. Tie with square knot; trim ends of yarn to ⅜''.

18. To make tail, cut nine 48'' lengths of green yarn. Thread needle with each length of yarn to make double strand and stitch through quilt at tail spot, pulling yarn halfway through quilt. Cut needle free. Attach all nine lengths of yarn at tail spot in this way to make 36 yarn ends, each 12'' long. Divide into three sections and braid to 6'' length. Tie securely and trim tassel 2'' long.

baby elephant pillow

MATERIALS

Aqua-checked gingham scrap, 13x17'' (¼'' checks)
White batiste, 13x17''
⅜ yard solid green fabric (or scraps left from quilt)
Bright pink scrap, 2¼x2¼''
Green yarn, 20 yards, 3-ply sport weight
Pink yarn, 1½ yards
Black yarn, 1½ yards
Baby pillow, 12x16''

DIRECTIONS

Finished pillowcover fits a standard baby pillow, 12x16''. The pattern is half the actual size; each square in the pattern = 1 square inch.

1. Enlarge the pattern following directions in How-to Section. Note that trunk curve is sharper than head and rump curve.

2. Cut out patterns for pillow front, ear, cheek and toes. Cut pillow back pattern in two pieces, indicated by dotted lines. (In finished pillowcover, the back pieces overlap so you can easily stuff pillow inside.) *Pattern line is stitching line.*

3. Lay gingham right side up over batiste lining and treat as one fabric. Pin or tape pattern to front of gingham, matching pattern edges with edge of checks for neatest results. With basting thread or light pencil line, trace around pattern. Cut out pillow top, adding ¼'' seam allowance.

4. Mark positions for features: trunk, toes, cheek, ear and eye (see transfer directions in How-to Section). Baste along (but not on) trunk and head lines, to hold gingham and batiste together.

5. On wrong side of green fabric, trace around the two pattern pieces for pillow back (elephant facing right). Add ¼'' seam allowance around outside edge, and ¾'' hem allowance for overlap; cut out. Fold green fabric and cut ear front and back together, adding ¼'' seam allowance all around. Set aside until needed.

6. From remaining green fabric, cut nine toes, adding ¼'' hem allowance around each toe. Turn under hem allowance on curved edge only; finger-press and baste. Pin toes in place along lower edge of pillow top and baste along seam line. Sew curved edge of toes to pillow top, first with invisible hand stitches, then with green yarn blanket stitches. (See embroidery stitches in How-to Section.)

7. With green yarn, chain-stitch leg lines, and blanket-stitch trunk line.

8. Cut out pink cheek, adding ¼'' hem allowance. Turn under hem, finger-press and baste. Sew in place on pillow top, first with invisible hand stitches, then with pink yarn blanket stitches.

9. Embroider black eye in satin stitch.

10. Turn under ¾'' hem allowances on green back pieces of pillowcover; turn under ¼'' on cut edges to make ½'' hems. Pin hems; machine stitch; remove pins.

11. Pin back pieces to pillow top, right sides together. Back pieces overlap at center. Baste; machine stitch ¼'' from edge, all around pillowcover. Remove pins; trim seams; clip curves.

12. Turn pillowcover right side out. Pin all around outside edge to position seam line exactly on edge; baste; remove pins. Blanket-stitch around entire outer edge.

13. Pin ear front to ear back, right sides together; machine stitch ¼'' from edge, leaving 2'' opening. Remove pins; clip curves; trim corners.

14. Turn ear right side out; close opening with hand stitches. Pin all around ear to position seam line exactly on edge; baste; remove pins.

15. Pin ear in place and sew to pillow top along head line only with invisible hand stitches. Remove pins. With green yarn, blanket-stitch along head line; continue blanket stitch to meet trunk line. Finish remaining three edges of ear with blanket stitch.

16. Make baby elephant's tail same as mother's, using three pieces of yarn 30'' long. This makes a tail of twelve strands, 7½'' long. Braid 3'', tie securely and trim tassel 2'' long.

17. Insert pillow.

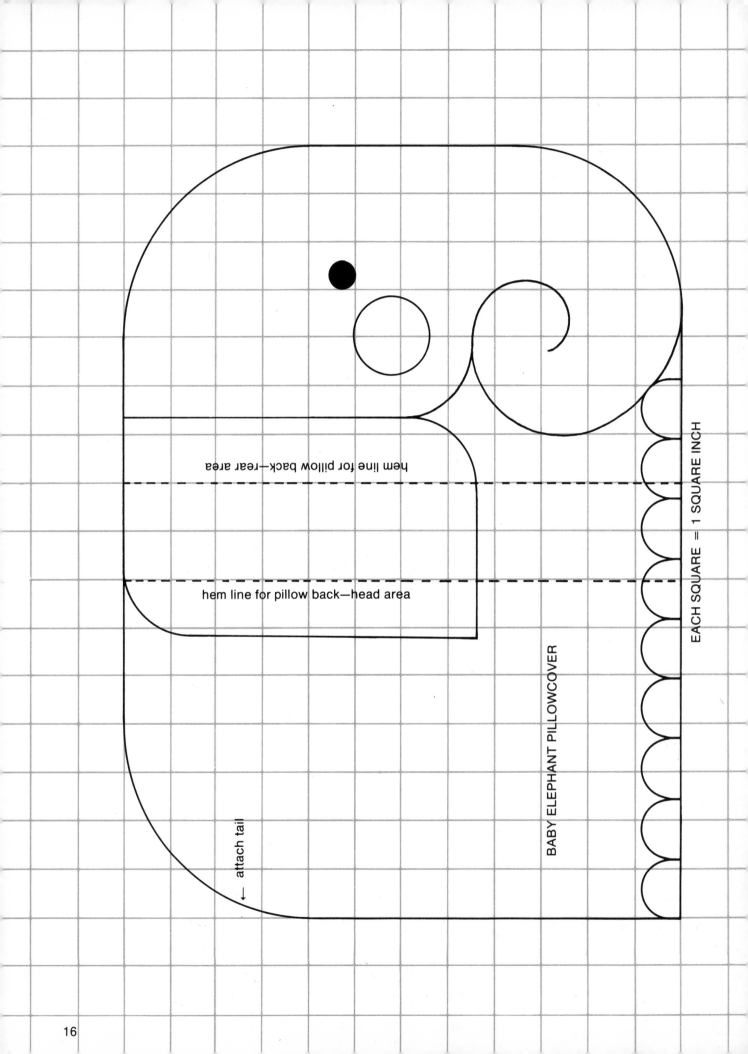

hem line for pillow back—rear area

hem line for pillow back—head area

attach tail

BABY ELEPHANT PILLOWCOVER

EACH SQUARE = 1 SQUARE INCH

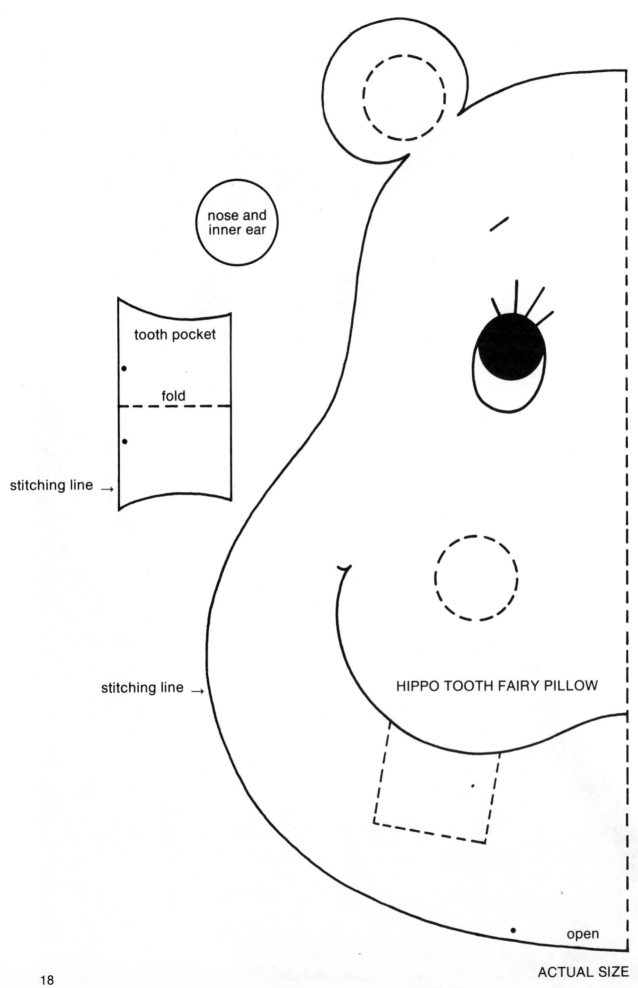

nose and inner ear

tooth pocket

fold

stitching line →

stitching line →

HIPPO TOOTH FAIRY PILLOW

open

ACTUAL SIZE

18

My niece's note to the tooth fairy inspired this hippo pillow design. You'll want to start sewing one as soon as your youngster shows you how his tooth wiggles.

When it falls out, tuck it into one of the hippo's tooth pockets—he's guaranteed not to swallow it.

For the payment, a coin as big as a quarter can go into each of the tooth pockets . . . but if the bounty ever goes above 50¢, we're in big trouble!

DeaR TOOTH
FaiRY
i LOST MY
TOOTH BUt
i ZWAL O W ED
iT
EMILY

HIPPO PILLOW

MATERIALS

Pink, red and white geometric
   print fabric, 11x20''
White scrap, 4x6'' (batiste)
Pink scrap, 1½x3''
Red scrap, 1½x3''
Red, black and white embroidery
   thread
Polyester stuffing

DIRECTIONS

1. Pattern is actual size—copy it on folded tracing paper to make complete hippo head. Cut out. Cut out patterns for teeth and nose. *Pattern line is stitching line.*

2. Pin head pattern to wrong side of fabric. Trace lightly with pencil or ball-point pen. Baste along tracing line to get pattern outline to right side of fabric, but do not cut out yet.

3. Mark positions for features (see transfer directions in How-to Section).

4. From folded pink fabric, cut nose pieces, adding ⅛'' seam allowance. From folded red fabric, cut inner ear pieces, adding ⅛'' seam allowance.

5. Turn under hem allowances, finger-press and baste. Pin and sew nose and ear pieces in place, using invisible hand stitches; remove pins. Blanket-stitch edges, using two strands red embroidery thread (see How-to section for stitches).

6. With two strands black embroidery thread, chain-stitch eyebrows, eyelashes and eye shape; fill in eye with white and black satin stitch, using three strands thread. Chain-stitch mouth with six strands red embroidery thread.

7. Fold white fabric, right sides together, and trace tooth pocket outline twice. Stitch around outline of each one, leaving ¾'' opening on long side. Cut out each one, ⅛'' from stitching line. Trim corners; clip curves; turn right side out. Close opening with invisible hand stitches and press.

8. Blanket-stitch one curved edge of tooth using two strands of white embroidery thread. Pin opposite curved edge to face below smile line (see pattern for placement). Blanket-stitch this edge directly to face. Fold tooth and blanket-stitch sides to form open pocket. Remove pins.

9. Lay hippo face over matching fabric for back of pillow, right sides together. Machine stitch around outline, leaving seam open 3'' at chin. Cut out ¼'' from stitching line (⅛'' around ears). Clip curves; clip into V-angles at each side of ears.

10. Turn right side out. Use a blunt tool (crochet hook) to push out ears. Machine stitch across lower ears to prevent stuffing from entering. Stuff. Close opening at chin with invisible hand stitches.

Baths will be more fun if the washcloth is an animal your child can talk to. These washcloth hand puppets all have pouches to carry the individual-size soaps that travelers bring home from motels.

DIRECTIONS FOR ALL PUPPETS

1. Trace actual-size patterns on tracing paper, adding additional length for soap pocket—2¼'' below dotted line. Fold pattern up on dotted line and trace curve under arms. Cut out pattern.

2. Pin pattern to terry side of washcloth with lower edge along finished edge of cloth. Trace pattern outline; mark fold line. Baste along tracing outline to transfer animal shape to velour side of cloth. Do not cut out puppet until after stitching (step 6).

3. Pin pattern to velour side and mark face details on fabric. (Best way is to cut away these details in your pattern, so you can use it as a template.)

4. Trace patterns for appliques and cut from fabric adding ⅛'' hem allowance. Turn under hem allowance; baste; pin in place on puppet face and sew with invisible hand stitches. Complete embroidery (see How-to Section for stitches).

5. Fold on pocket line and baste.

6. Lay embroidered puppet face down on terry side of second washcloth, lining up folded edge with finished edge of second washcloth. Pin edges. Machine stitch on outline, leaving bottom open. Remove pins. Cut out puppet, trimming seam to ⅛''. Clip curves; clip into V-angles; trim corners. Turn right side out. Topstitch edge all around, leaving bottom open.

WASHCLOTH PUPPETS

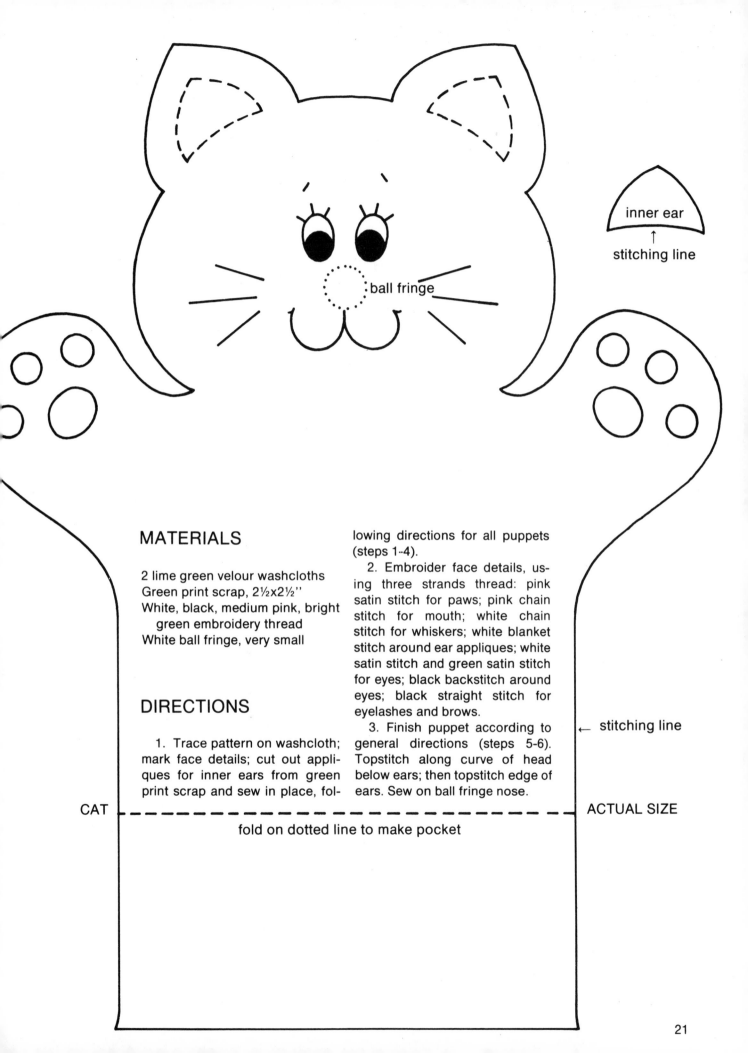

inner ear

↑
stitching line

ball fringe

MATERIALS

2 lime green velour washcloths
Green print scrap, 2½x2½''
White, black, medium pink, bright
  green embroidery thread
White ball fringe, very small

DIRECTIONS

1. Trace pattern on washcloth; mark face details; cut out appliques for inner ears from green print scrap and sew in place, following directions for all puppets (steps 1-4).

2. Embroider face details, using three strands thread: pink satin stitch for paws; pink chain stitch for mouth; white chain stitch for whiskers; white blanket stitch around ear appliques; white satin stitch and green satin stitch for eyes; black backstitch around eyes; black straight stitch for eyelashes and brows.

3. Finish puppet according to general directions (steps 5-6). Topstitch along curve of head below ears; then topstitch edge of ears. Sew on ball fringe nose.

← stitching line

CAT

ACTUAL SIZE

fold on dotted line to make pocket

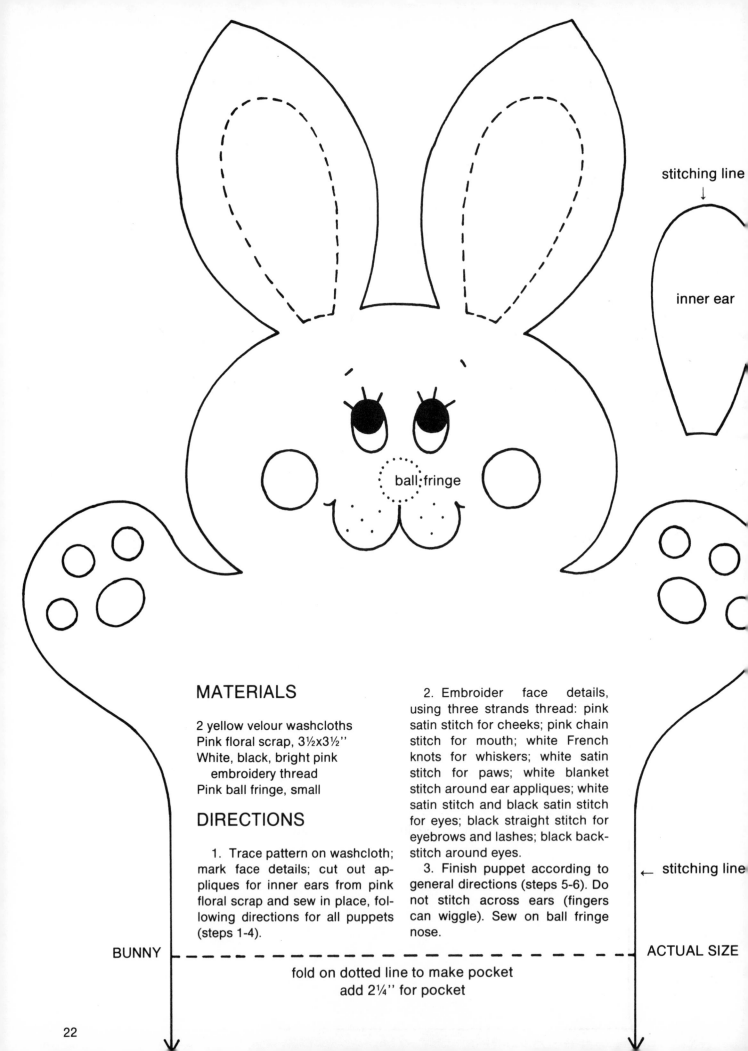

stitching line
↓

inner ear

ball fringe

MATERIALS

2 yellow velour washcloths
Pink floral scrap, 3½x3½''
White, black, bright pink
   embroidery thread
Pink ball fringe, small

DIRECTIONS

1. Trace pattern on washcloth; mark face details; cut out appliques for inner ears from pink floral scrap and sew in place, following directions for all puppets (steps 1-4).

2. Embroider face details, using three strands thread: pink satin stitch for cheeks; pink chain stitch for mouth; white French knots for whiskers; white satin stitch for paws; white blanket stitch around ear appliques; white satin stitch and black satin stitch for eyes; black straight stitch for eyebrows and lashes; black back-stitch around eyes.

3. Finish puppet according to general directions (steps 5-6). Do not stitch across ears (fingers can wiggle). Sew on ball fringe nose.

← stitching line

BUNNY

ACTUAL SIZE

fold on dotted line to make pocket
add 2¼'' for pocket

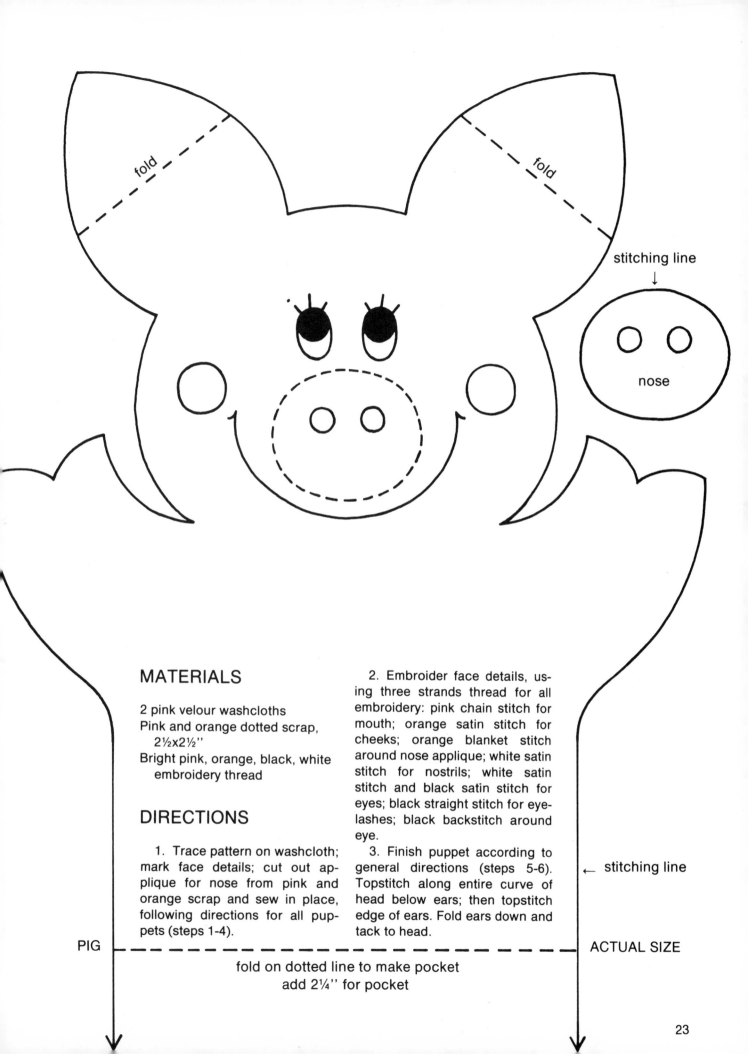

fold

fold

stitching line

nose

MATERIALS

2 pink velour washcloths
Pink and orange dotted scrap,
 2½x2½''
Bright pink, orange, black, white
 embroidery thread

DIRECTIONS

1. Trace pattern on washcloth; mark face details; cut out applique for nose from pink and orange scrap and sew in place, following directions for all puppets (steps 1-4).

2. Embroider face details, using three strands thread for all embroidery: pink chain stitch for mouth; orange satin stitch for cheeks; orange blanket stitch around nose applique; white satin stitch for nostrils; white satin stitch and black satin stitch for eyes; black straight stitch for eyelashes; black backstitch around eye.

3. Finish puppet according to general directions (steps 5-6). Topstitch along entire curve of head below ears; then topstitch edge of ears. Fold ears down and tack to head.

← stitching line

PIG

ACTUAL SIZE

fold on dotted line to make pocket
add 2¼'' for pocket

23

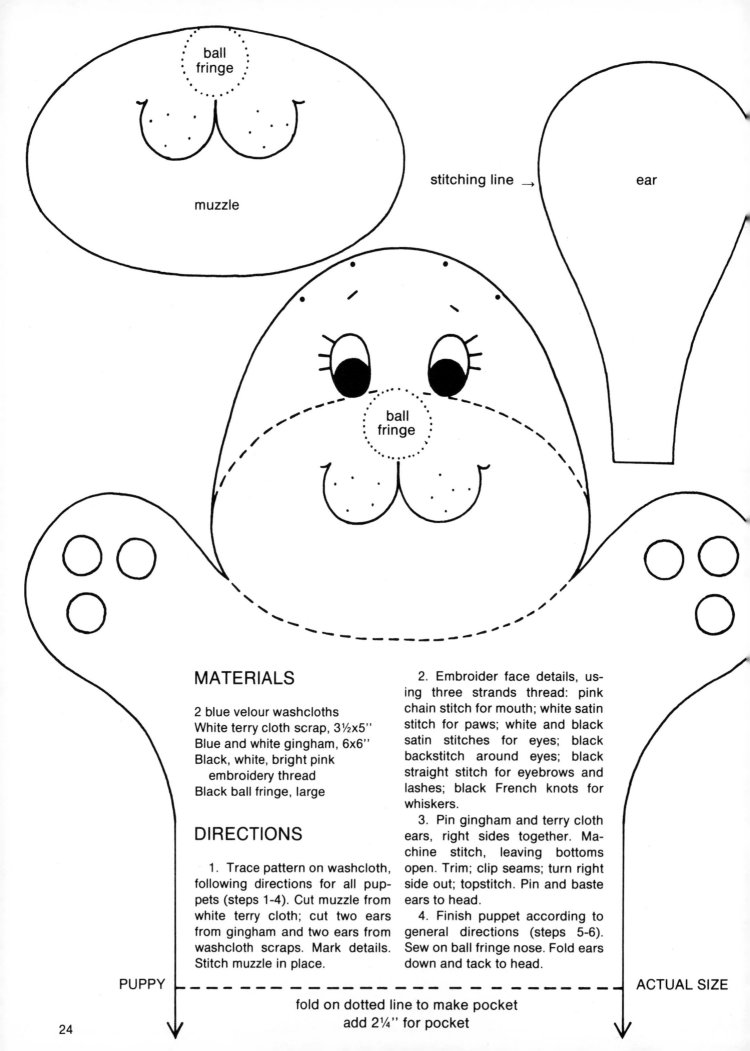

ball
fringe

muzzle

stitching line →   ear

ball
fringe

MATERIALS

2 blue velour washcloths
White terry cloth scrap, 3½x5''
Blue and white gingham, 6x6''
Black, white, bright pink
  embroidery thread
Black ball fringe, large

DIRECTIONS

1. Trace pattern on washcloth, following directions for all puppets (steps 1-4). Cut muzzle from white terry cloth; cut two ears from gingham and two ears from washcloth scraps. Mark details. Stitch muzzle in place.

2. Embroider face details, using three strands thread: pink chain stitch for mouth; white satin stitch for paws; white and black satin stitches for eyes; black backstitch around eyes; black straight stitch for eyebrows and lashes; black French knots for whiskers.

3. Pin gingham and terry cloth ears, right sides together. Machine stitch, leaving bottoms open. Trim; clip seams; turn right side out; topstitch. Pin and baste ears to head.

4. Finish puppet according to general directions (steps 5-6). Sew on ball fringe nose. Fold ears down and tack to head.

PUPPY   ACTUAL SIZE

fold on dotted line to make pocket
add 2¼'' for pocket

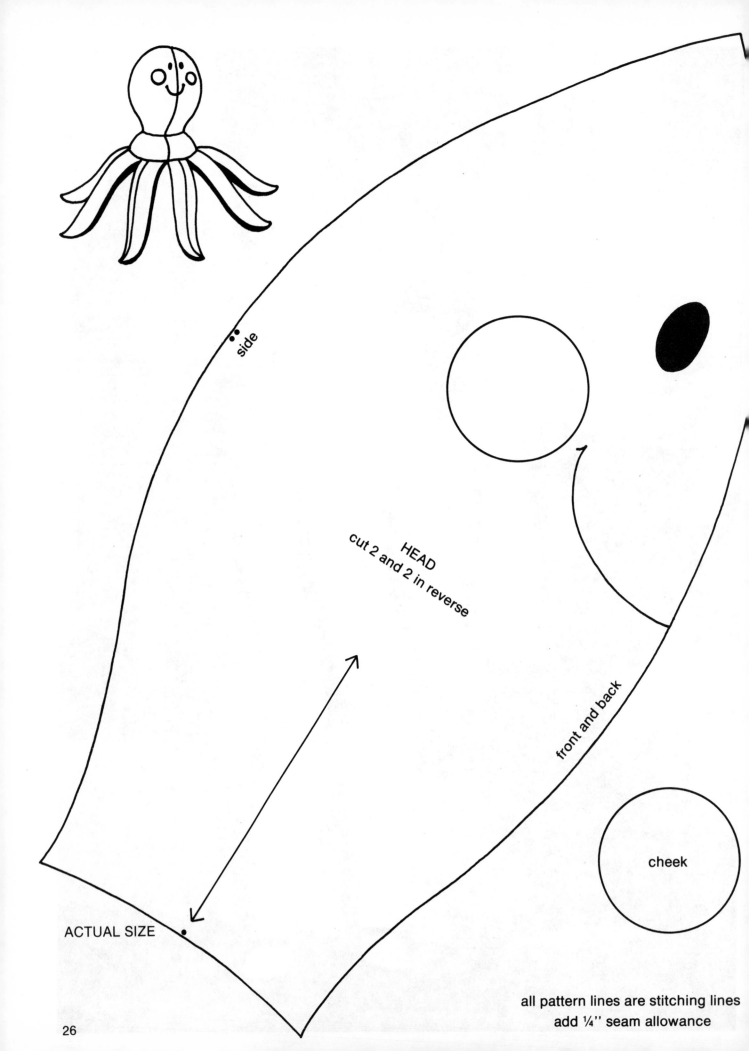

side

HEAD
cut 2 and 2 in reverse

front and back

cheek

ACTUAL SIZE

all pattern lines are stitching lines
add ¼'' seam allowance

26

Every time I present Ozzie the Octopus to my two- and three-year-old neighbors, he makes a big hit. Watch a child play with this giant stuffed toy and you'll see why. Ozzie is very huggable and loves to ride on shoulders. He's also fun to hide under, peeking out through his eight curved arms.

Ozzie's interesting silhouette is the result of some precise seaming.

We give actual-size patterns for the tentacles so they'll have exactly the right curve. The head is seamed separately, then joined to the neck with hand stitches. Ozzie wears a tie to cover the stitches.

Dimensional toys like this are a little more difficult to sew than flat designs. But look at the sketches; they'll help you understand exactly what to do.

OCTOPUS

MATERIALS

1 yard solid color fabric
   for underbody
⅞ yard contrasting color or print
   fabric (45'' wide) for upper body
White pique, 14x14'' (or other
   medium-weight fabric) for hat
Print fabric, 4½x30'' for scarf
Red or pink fabric scrap, 5x2½''
Black and red (or bright pink)
   embroidery thread
Polyester stuffing

DIRECTIONS

Underbody pattern, when completed, measures 33½'' from tentacle to tentacle. It looks like a sunburst (see sketch, page 29).

1. Trace patterns for underbody tentacle and tentacle tip, butting them together on dotted lines to make one complete outline. Use this tracing to complete pattern for underbody.

2. In the center of paper 34x34'', trace a full circle 8⅝'' in diameter (underbody guide shows only half-circle). Trace eight tentacles radiating from circle as indicated by broken lines. Cut out entire pattern for underbody in one piece.

3. Trace actual-size patterns for head, neck, upper tentacle, hat and hat brim; cut out. *All pattern lines are stitching lines.*

4. Trace pattern for complete underbody on wrong side of fabric; cut out, adding ¼'' seam allowance.

5. Fold upper body fabric right sides together and trace patterns for head, neck and upper tentacles as shown on cutting layout. Cut out, adding ¼'' seam allowance. You will have four head pieces, four neck pieces and sixteen tentacles.

6. On one pair of head sections, trace face details on wrong sides of fabric; transfer markings to right sides by basting on tracing line.

7. Right sides together, pin the two face sections of head along undotted curve; stitch; clip curve. Repeat with remaining two head sections to make back of head. Right sides together, pin front of head to back along dotted curve; stitch, going over top of head in one continuous seam. Clip curve. Turn head right side out; stuff firmly; set aside.

8. Right sides together, stitch four neck pieces one to the next, making a ring. Clip curves; set aside.

9. Right sides together, stitch each pair of upper tentacle pieces along curve marked with a dot, matching dots. Clip curve.

10. Pin upper tentacles to lower (wider) edge of neck ring, placing each tentacle between a side seam and a dot—you'll have two tentacles within each quarter section of neck ring. Stitch tentacles to neck ring, right sides together. Clip curves.

11. Pin neck and upper tentacles to underbody, right sides together. Baste, easing fullness of upper tentacles. Machine stitch around entire sunburst shape in one continuous seam. Clip curves; clip into V-angles where tentacles meet neck; clip tips of tentacles; turn right side out. Stuff tentacles firmly; stuff neck area.

12. Fold under seam allowance at neck opening; baste. Insert stuffed head in neck opening; pin and stitch together very securely by hand using double thread.

13. Cut out pink cheeks; turn under seam allowance and pin to head. (Correct placement of facial features, if necessary—sometimes stuffing the head makes the smile crooked.) Use six full strands embroidery thread for all embroidery. With pink or red thread, applique cheeks to head with blanket stitches; chain-stitch mouth. Satin-stitch black eyes.

14. To make arms of octopus floppy, sew on seam line where tentacles meet neck, passing needle through to underbody. Use strong double thread for this line of ''quilting.''

15. Cut out scarf (measurements on pattern page) adding ¼'' seam allowance. Fold lengthwise, right sides together; pin and stitch, leaving a 2'' opening. Turn right side out and close opening by hand. Press; tie around neck of octopus.

16. Trace patterns for hat on white pique—four crowns, two brims. Cut out, adding ¼'' seam allowance. Right sides together, join two crown pieces; join remaining two crown pieces; stitch and clip curves. Pin front crown to back crown; stitch; clip curve. Press seam open; on right side, topstitch ⅛'' on each side of seam lines, stitching through seam allowance.

17. Stitch side seam of one hat brim to make ring; press seam open. Repeat for second brim. Right sides together, stitch one brim to the other, along outside edge. Clip

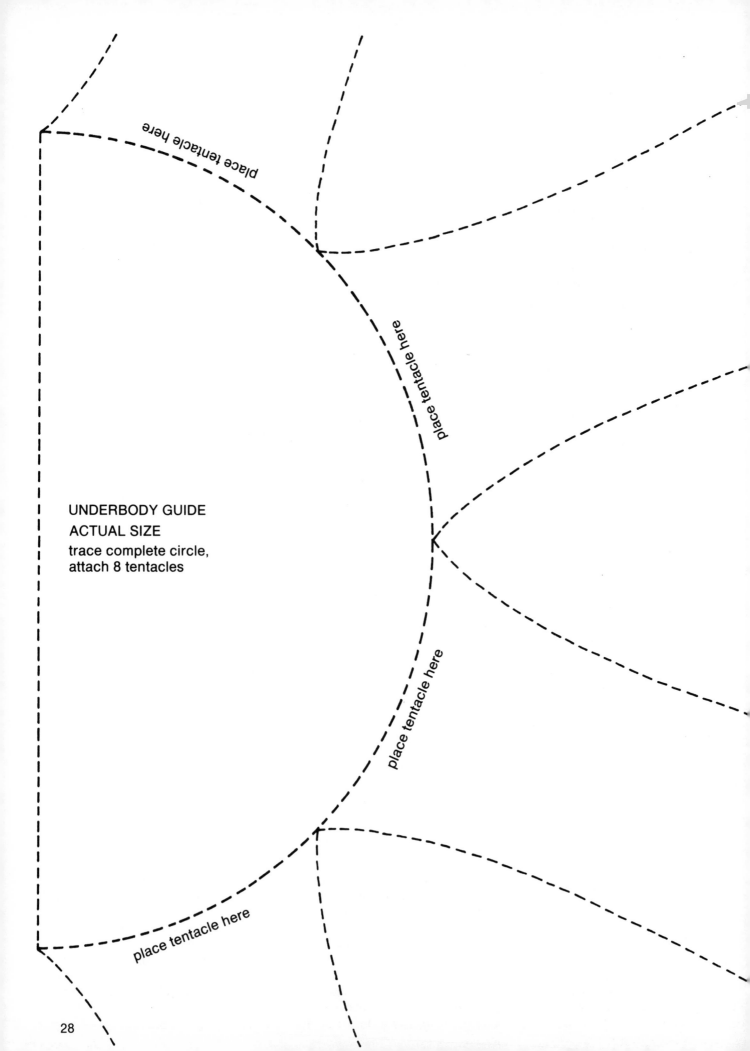

**UNDERBODY GUIDE
ACTUAL SIZE**
trace complete circle,
attach 8 tentacles

place tentacle here

place tentacle here

place tentacle here

place tentacle here

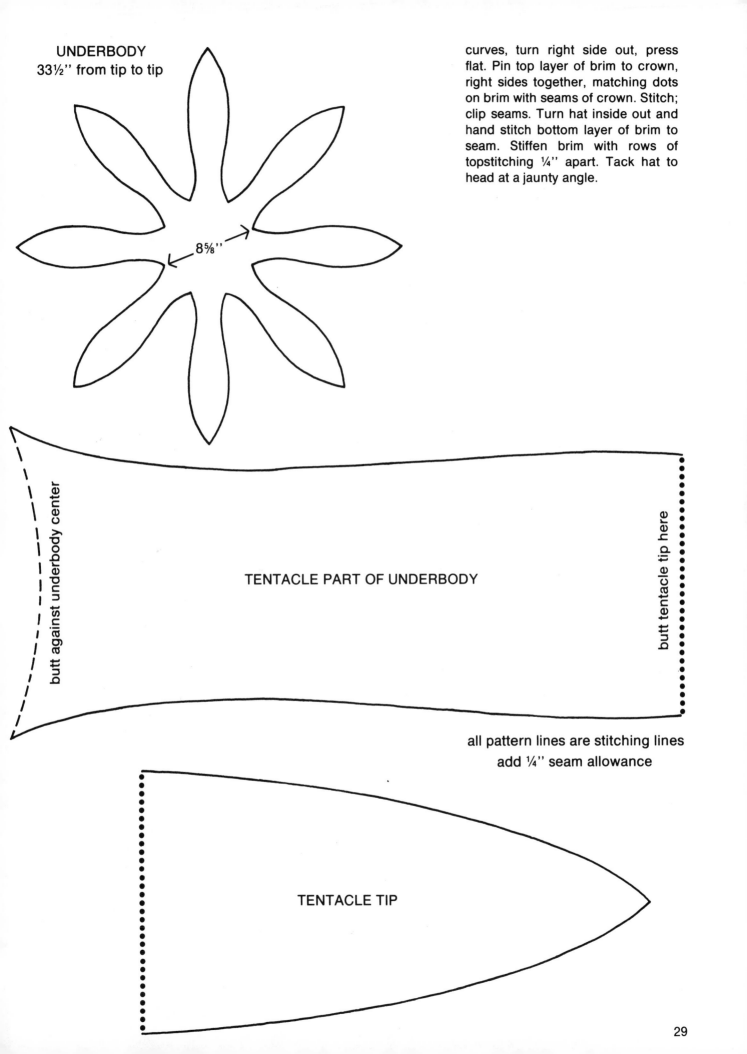

UNDERBODY
33½'' from tip to tip

8⅝''

curves, turn right side out, press flat. Pin top layer of brim to crown, right sides together, matching dots on brim with seams of crown. Stitch; clip seams. Turn hat inside out and hand stitch bottom layer of brim to seam. Stiffen brim with rows of topstitching ¼'' apart. Tack hat to head at a jaunty angle.

TENTACLE PART OF UNDERBODY

butt against underbody center

butt tentacle tip here

all pattern lines are stitching lines
add ¼'' seam allowance

TENTACLE TIP

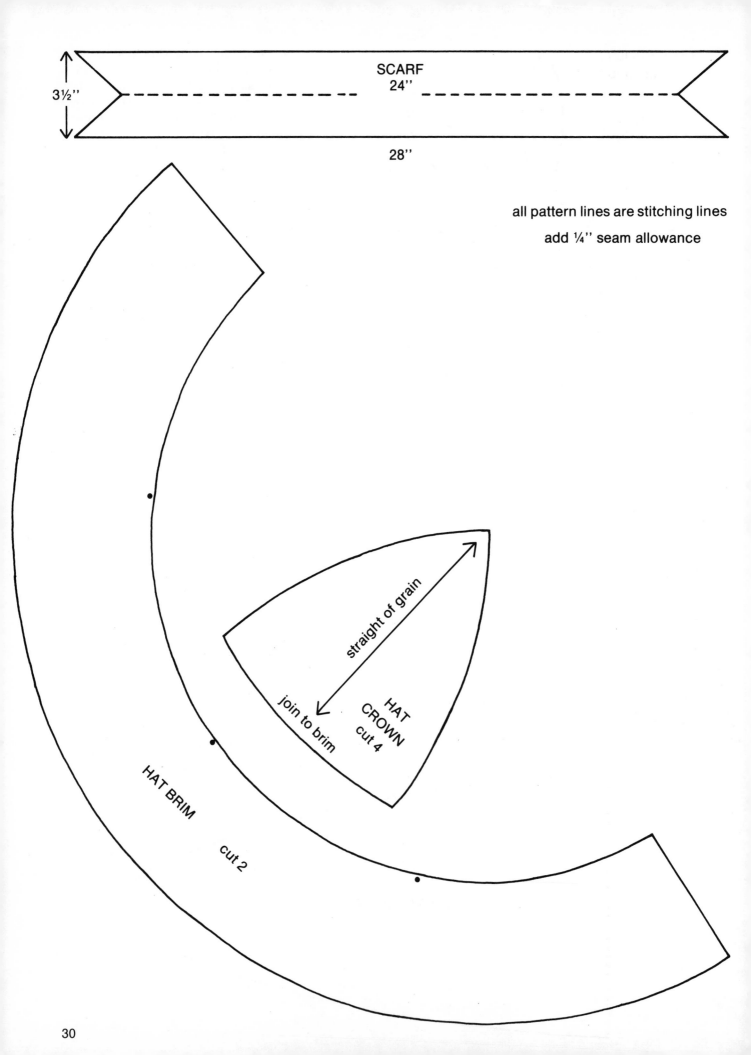

SCARF
24''

3½''

28''

all pattern lines are stitching lines

add ¼'' seam allowance

straight of grain

join to brim

HAT
CROWN
cut 4

HAT BRIM

cut 2

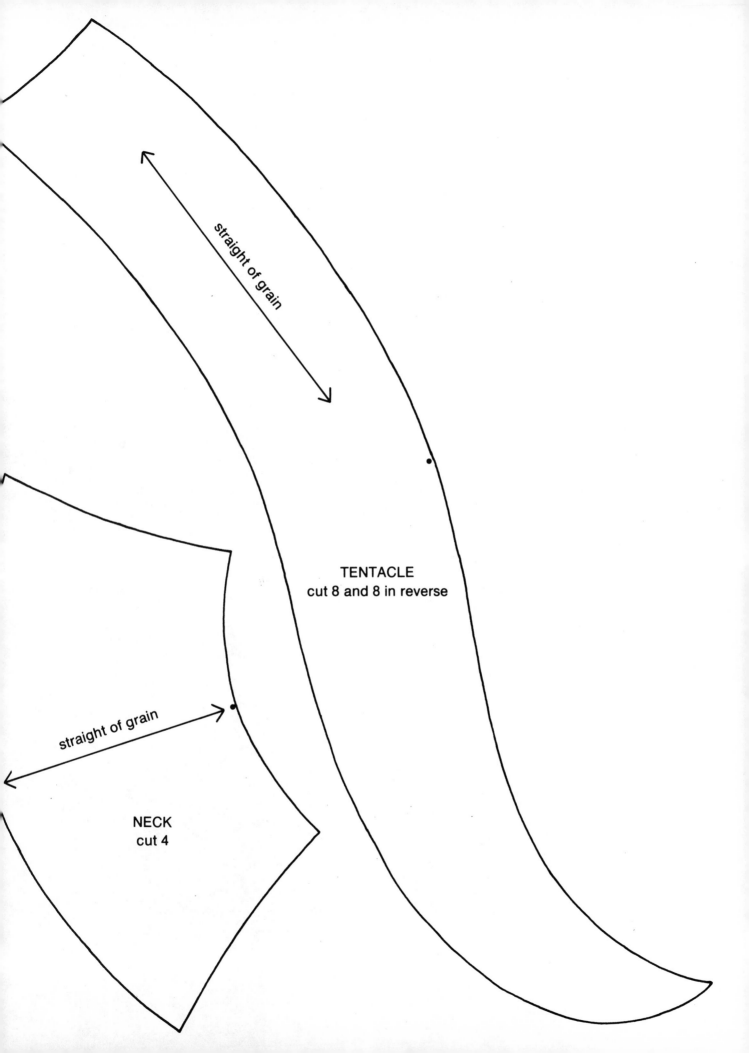

straight of grain

TENTACLE
cut 8 and 8 in reverse

straight of grain

NECK
cut 4

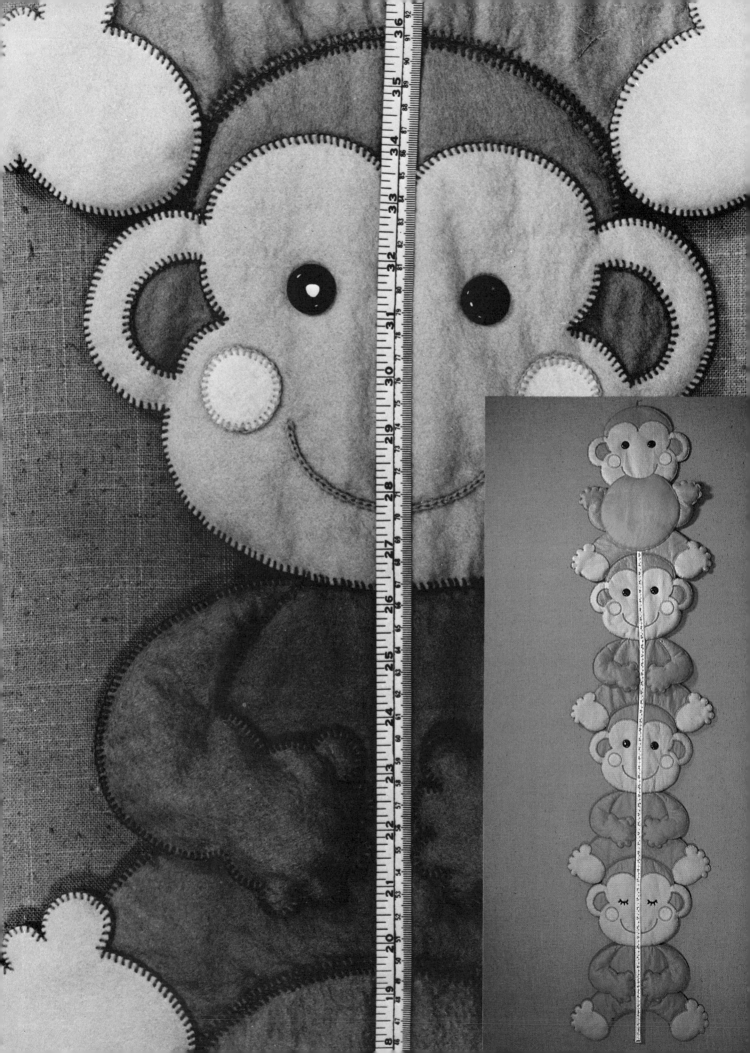

Four hungry monkeys are stacked up here, waiting their turn to bite into a jumbo lollipop with a tape measure stick. The lowest monkey on the stack knows he has a long wait, so he's taking a nap!

If you're making this growth chart for a very young child, I'd suggest embroidered instead of button eyes—so they can't be pulled off.

Padding the chart with polyester quilt batting gives the monkeys a soft roundness that is appealing. I've listed the batting as optional—but I believe the chart hangs better if it is padded—or at least stiffened with interfacing. If you are skillful at squeezing patterns onto fabric, you can cut out monkeys and backing from one yard of brown felt. Felt has no grain so the arms can be turned every which way to make best use of every scrap.

You can stitch this chart on the sewing machine if you prefer. Or you might replace the blanket stitch embroidery with the running stitch to speed the work.

MONKEY GROWTH CHART

MATERIALS

1⅛ yard medium or light brown felt (72'' wide)
¼ yard beige felt (or 6 pieces 9x12'')
Red-orange felt, 2 pieces 9x12''
Crewel embroidery yarn (3-ply):
    30 yards medium brown; 1 yard red-orange; 4 yards bright pink; 1 yard black
6 shiny black buttons (⅞'' diameter)
Thin polyester quilt batting (optional, but desirable)
Tape measure, 60'' (152 cm)

DIRECTIONS

1. Patterns for parts of monkey are all actual size; they can be fitted together as you trace them. Fold tracing paper 17x20'' lengthwise. Trace right half of monkey head and body; trace left half on other side of fold; cut out entire monkey outline. Trace complete lollipop pattern (right and left sides) the same way. Trace separate patterns for monkey face, cheeks, arms and feet.

2. To make pattern for backing: trace outline made by butting the head of one monkey against the leg curve of the next (see diagram).

3. Pin backing pattern to medium brown felt, laying pattern close to edge across the 72'' width. Trace around pattern; cut out shape carefully on outline. Avoid cutting into negative areas. Felt has no grain, so you can squeeze all the arms into scrap areas.

4. On remaining felt, trace four individual monkey outlines, plus sixteen arms—eight of them in reverse; cut out.

5. From beige felt, cut four faces and eight feet—four of the feet in reverse. Transfer markings for facial features following directions in How-to Section.

6. Cut out pink felt cheeks. Pin to face and applique with pink blanket stitches.

7. With double strand of black yarn, chain-stitch closed eyes for bottom monkey; embroider eye lashes with straight stitch. Sew black button eyes on other monkey faces (or embroider round eyes with satin stitch).

8. Cut out inner ears on monkey faces and baste faces to heads.

9. Baste beige feet to legs as shown by dotted lines.

10. Pin two arm pieces together, right sides out. With brown yarn, blanket-stitch around arm and hand, leaving arm open along dotted line. Stuff lightly with scraps of polyester batting. Repeat for remaining seven arms.

11. Attach arms to monkeys: line up top of arm at neck and let body overlap arm along dotted line. Pin and baste. (Lower arm lays over tummy.)

12. Pin pattern for backing to polyester batting; trace entire outline with a felt-tip pen. Remove pattern and cut out batting ¼'' *inside* pattern outline. Baste batting to wrong side of felt backing.

13. With batting sandwiched between, pin monkeys to backing, the sleepy monkey on the bottom. Fit curve of head against curve of legs and whipstitch these curves together without overlapping them.

14. Sew backing to back of arms along dotted lines.

15. Join monkeys to backing with blanket stitches. Use brown yarn; blanket-stitch under chins, around top of heads and along leg curves. Also use blanket stitches to applique beige feet and faces, around inner ears and along brow lines.

16. Place assembled chart on the floor and use a ruler and ball-point pen to draw a perpendicular line through the center of the bottom three monkeys—use the point of the

ACTUAL SIZE

ARM

insert in body seam

cut out

FACE

place on fold

34

ACTUAL SIZE

all pattern lines are cutting lines

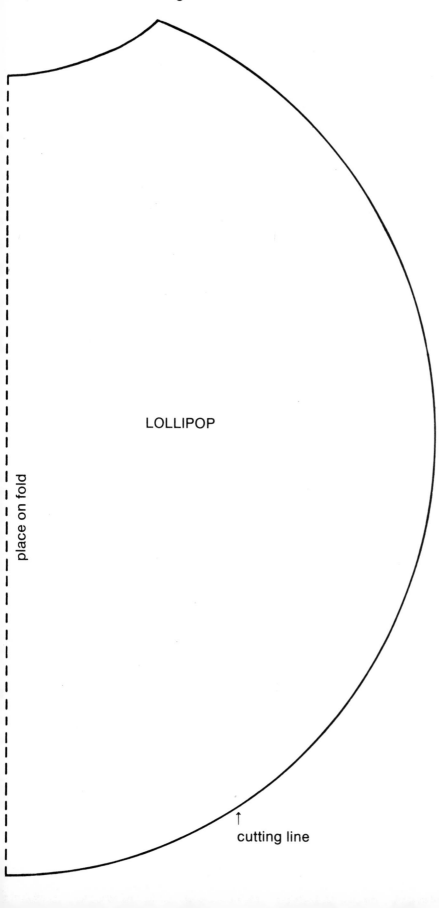

LOLLIPOP

place on fold

↑
cutting line

brow as a guide. Do not mark top monkey.

17. Lay tape measure over this line so that low numbered end is even with the feet of the bottom monkey; tape will extend about 3⅛" below leg curve. Use masking tape to hold it in place while stitching. Match needle thread to tape measure and machine stitch with large stitches.

18. From red-orange felt, cut out two lollipops. Trace lollipop pattern on polyester batting; cut out batting ¼" *inside* pattern outline.

19. Sandwich batting between lollipop front and back; pin. With red-orange yarn, blanket-stitch around edge of lollipop except in bite area—baste bite edges together.

20. Pin lollipop to top monkey exactly on smile line; sew with invisible hand stitches. Then embroider smile with chain stitch using double strand of pink yarn, and catching edge of lollipop with your stitches. Chain-stitch pink smiles on three bottom monkeys, too.

21. Fold elbows of top monkey to back of chart to put hands in up position; tack in place on back. Sew lollipop to arms and tummy with invisible hand stitches.

22. Tack hands of bottom three monkeys so fingers touch tape measure.

23. To hang growth chart, sew three small rings or yarn loops to backing behind ears and head of top monkey.

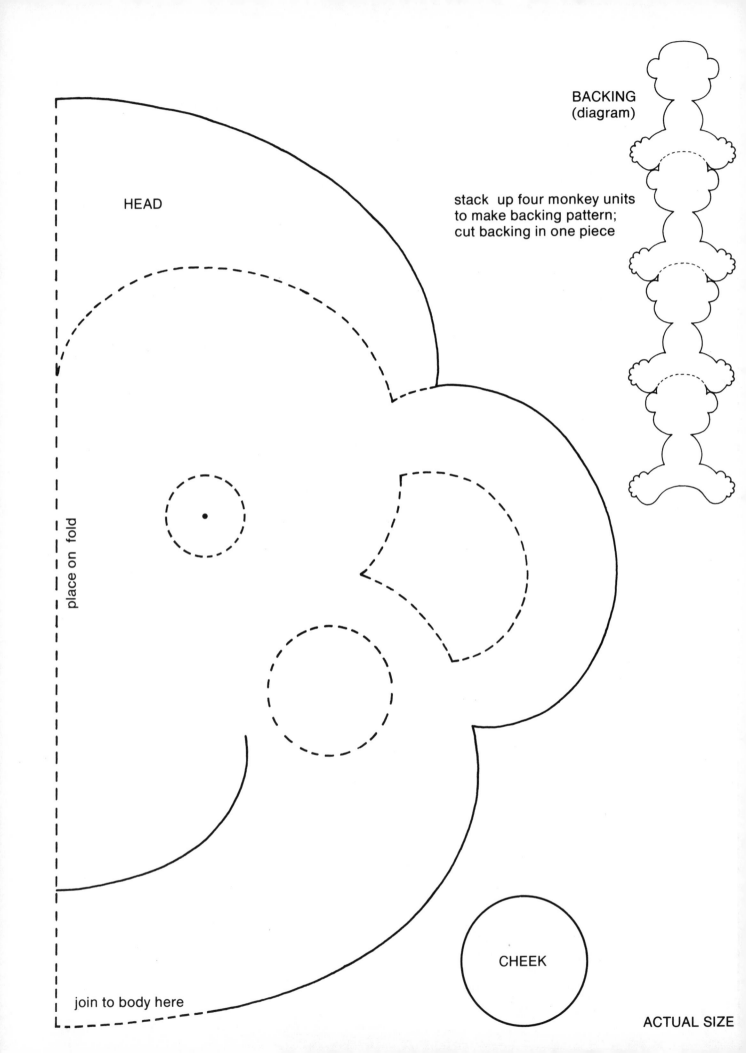

HEAD

BACKING
(diagram)

stack up four monkey units
to make backing pattern;
cut backing in one piece

place on fold

join to body here

CHEEK

ACTUAL SIZE

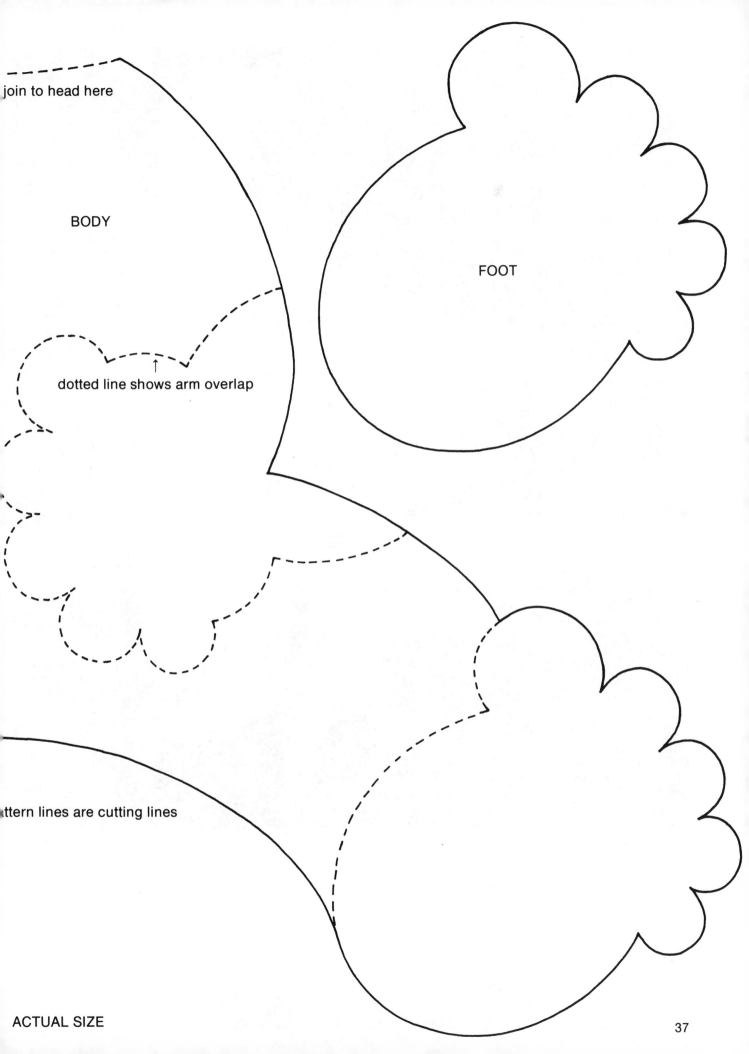

join to head here

BODY

dotted line shows arm overlap

FOOT

ttern lines are cutting lines

ACTUAL SIZE

37

PENCIL
DUFFEL BAG

You can pack quite a bit of lightweight gear into this stubby pencil bag (your needlework, for instance). It's about 22" long from point to eraser. It could be personalized with applique black letters on one of the panels. If you don't have use for a bag, omit the handles and zipper and stuff the pencil to make a bolster pillow.

MATERIALS

⅝ yard yellow fabric (45" wide)
½ yard polka dot fabric (45" wide)
   for lining
Black fabric, 8x32"
Rust fabric, 11x42"
Beige fabric, 11½x18"
Polyester batting, 28x38"
   medium or heavy weight
9" black zipper (neckline type)
Black bias tape, single-fold, 3 yards

DIRECTIONS

All pencil parts are shown in miniature on page 41, labeled with actual-size dimensions. There are actual-size patterns for the pointed end of the pencil.

1. Trace actual-size pattern for black pencil tip. Trace the quarter section of pencil point, adding three more sections to make complete pattern.

2. On tracing paper, draw actual-size patterns with dimensions as labeled for pencil stem, black band, eraser band and handles. Use a compass to make a circle 10" in diameter for eraser top. *All pattern lines are stitching lines.*

3. Cut pencil tip and band from black fabric; pencil point from beige; eraser band and top from rust; pencil stem and handles from yellow, adding ¼" seam allowance to all edges.

4. In seam allowance areas mark eraser top, eraser band, pencil stem and pencil point with dots to indicate quarter sections (see pattern). Later, you'll match dots when stitching pencil parts together.

5. Cut lining for pencil stem 15x31" plus ¼" for seam allowance. Use patterns to cut lining for pencil point and eraser top, adding ¼" seam allowance.

6. Cut batting, using the three lin-

ing pieces as patterns. Also cut two strips of batting 2x22½" for handles.

7. Make handles first. Turn under ¼" seam allowance on both long edges; press. Fold handle in half lengthwise, wrong sides together; press. Insert a strip of batting 2x22½" between folds; sew open edges together with invisible hand stitches. Quilt handle with seven parallel rows of machine stitching (large stitches) ¼" apart. Repeat for second handle. Set aside.

8. Cut five pieces of bias tape 10" long. Baste to right side of yellow pencil stem (see dotted lines on miniature pattern for placement). Baste center strip first; others are spaced approximately 4¾" apart.

9. Right sides together, pin black band to top of yellow pencil stem; stitch. Pin rust eraser band to black band; stitch. Press both seams open.

10. Sandwich batting between pencil lining and pencil, both right sides out. Pin all around edges. Baste layers together.

11. Attach handles. Pin ends of handles under black bias tape strips on pencil stem; see miniature pattern for placement. Handles should meet black band at top of pencil and should be positioned 2¼" from bottom (see sketch).

12. Stitch handle ends to pencil underneath the tape. Then top-

eraser band

black band

handle

bias tape

topstitch

2¼"

stitch all tapes, stitching through all layers down both sides of each strip of tape, to quilt bag.

13. Zipper is sewn in by hand after the raw edges (left and right) of yellow pencil stem are bound with black bias tape. To bind edges, machine stitch ⅜" from raw edge, catching layers of batting and lining. Trim to ⅛" and overcast edges. Cut two 10" lengths of bias tape. Fold in half lengthwise, encasing overcast edges of pencil stem. Baste; machine stitch.

14. Before setting in zipper, fold pencil, right sides together, and pin sides of eraser and black band; baste; machine stitch eraser and black band; leave pencil open for zipper. Press seam flat.

15. Turn pencil right side out. Butt together the two bias-bound edges and whipstitch with a colored thread that will be easy to see and remove. Center zipper under this whipstitched seam and sew zipper in place by hand. Remove whipstitching. Put pencil aside while you make pencil point.

16. Machine stitch curve of black tip on hem line. Clip curve; turn under hem allowance; baste. Pin black tip to beige pencil point; baste; machine stitch curved edge.

17. Sandwich batting between point and point lining, both right sides out. Baste.

18. Fold point, right sides together; pin; machine stitch straight seam to tip; trim seam at tip. Turn point right side out.

19. Turn pencil inside out and pin to point, right sides together, matching quarter-section dots. Baste point to pencil stem, easing in fullness. Machine stitch.

20. Sandwich batting between eraser top and lining, both right sides out. Baste.

21. Pin eraser top to eraser band, right sides together, matching quarter-section dots. Baste, easing in fullness; machine stitch. Turn entire pencil right side out.

22. By hand, sew black bias tape around pencil along seam line joining pencil and point.

23. From stiff paper, cut a circle 9½" in diameter and insert in eraser end, so pencil will hold its shape.

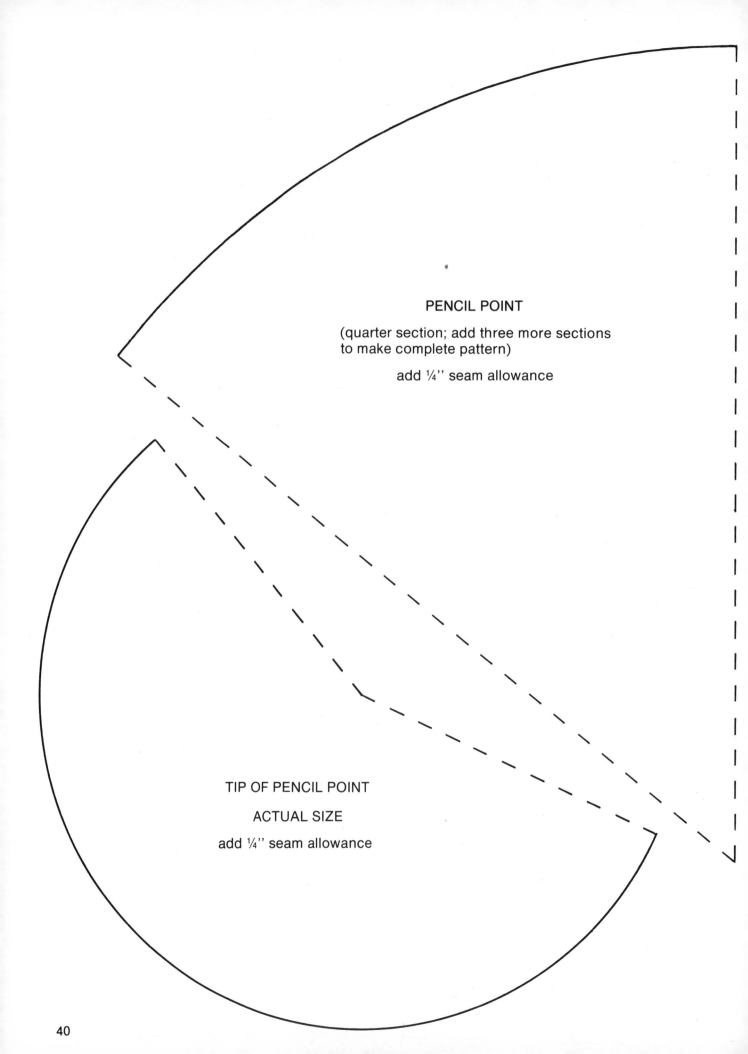

PENCIL POINT

(quarter section; add three more sections
to make complete pattern)

add ¼'' seam allowance

TIP OF PENCIL POINT

ACTUAL SIZE

add ¼'' seam allowance

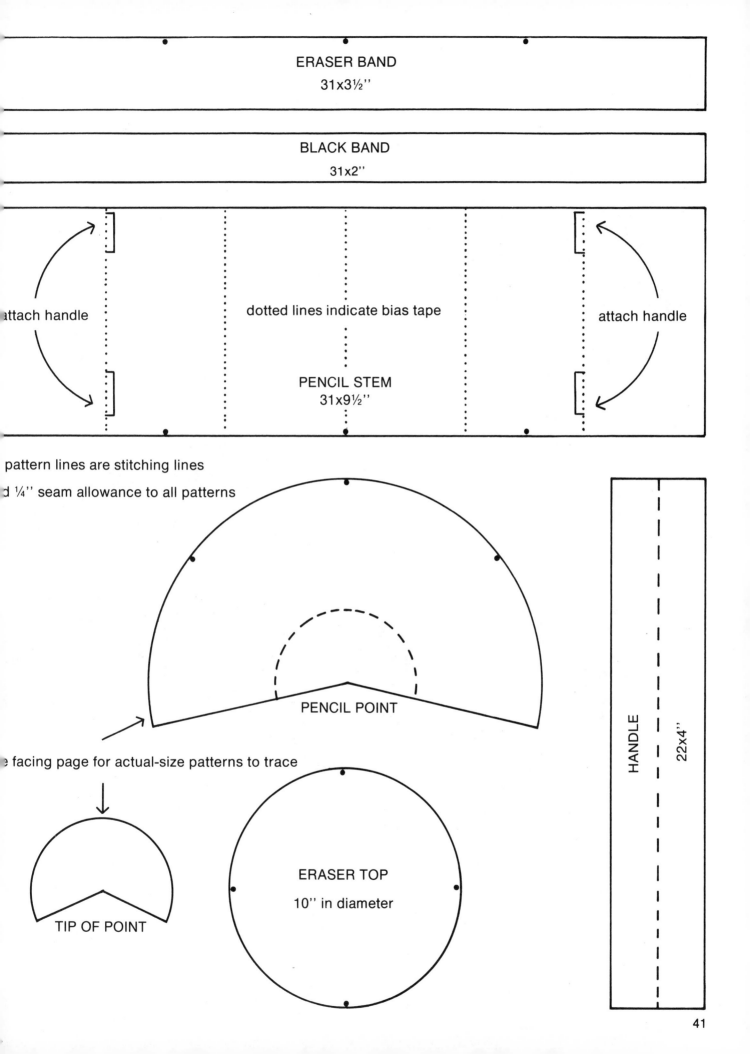

ERASER BAND
31x3½''

BLACK BAND
31x2''

attach handle

dotted lines indicate bias tape

attach handle

PENCIL STEM
31x9½''

pattern lines are stitching lines

d ¼'' seam allowance to all patterns

PENCIL POINT

e facing page for actual-size patterns to trace

HANDLE
22x4''

TIP OF POINT

ERASER TOP
10'' in diameter

This friendly lion holds a napkin in his paw pocket! He's especially helpful when he rides in on a bed tray—he's got a big smile for a youngster who eats a good breakfast.

You can also use this design for a pillow toy or quilt. Just stitch the paw down to the mane instead of making it a pocket. If you want to make a quilt, it's easy to blow the pattern outline up to crib size. Follow directions in step 2, using 3'' squares instead of 1'' squares, and fill in the V-area where the back and mane meet. Finished quilt will be approximately 33x54''.

I love to embroider, so I blanket-stitch the face details, around the face and mane and all the outer edges. If you want to speed up the job, use your sewing machine with zigzag stitch for quilting and edging the applique. Also, you can cut the applique pieces without hem allowances and use fusible web to attach cutouts to lion face; then zig-zag raw edges.

LION PLACEMAT

MATERIALS

½ yard yellow (with red) calico (45'' wide)
Red (with yellow) calico, 12x12''
White scrap, 5x5''
Black scrap, 2x3''
Red scrap, 2x4''
Yellow scrap, 13x13'', for napkin
Black embroidery thread
Polyester quilt batting, 12x23''
Black medium rickrack, 1 yard

DIRECTIONS

Finished placemat is approximately 11½x18''. The pattern is one-half actual size; each square in the pattern = 1 square inch. Pattern for lion face is actual size.

1. Trace and cut out patterns for lion face, ears, nose, cheeks. With a compass, draw circle 11½'' in diameter and cut out; this is actual-size pattern for mane.

2. To enlarge pattern for complete lion, draw 1'' squares on paper 12x22''; copy lines from small squares to corresponding large squares, using the squares as a drawing guide. (If you lay mane pattern in place on 1'' squares, you can draw around it . . . then, the rest is easy.) *Pattern lines are stitching lines.*

3. Fold yellow calico, trace pattern on wrong side and cut out lion front and back, adding ¼'' seam allowance. Cut head from yellow calico, mane from red calico; ears and upper nose from white scrap, cheeks from red scrap and nose from black scrap, adding ¼'' hem allowance all around each cutout.

4. Transfer markings for appliques and stitching lines (see transfer directions in How-to Section).

5. Use body as pattern to cut quilt batting with same ¼'' seam allowance.

6. Layer pieces in this order: batting; body back (right side up); body front (wrong side up). Carefully line up edges and pin. Machine stitch ¼'' from edge, leaving 4'' opening on bottom edge. Remove pins; clip curves; clip into V-angles; trim corners. Trim batting close to stitching line.

7. Turn placemat right side out; close opening with hand stitches. Pin all around outside edges to position seam line exactly on edges; baste, remove pins.

8. Turn under hem allowances for appliques; clip curves and V-angles as necessary; finger-press; baste. (See How-to Section for tips on handling small appliques.) Do not turn under lower, curved hem allowance of white nose piece.

9. Applique face details using invisible hand stitches (black nose overlaps white part). With three strands black embroidery thread, satin-stitch eyes and chain-stitch mouth. Applique face to mane.

10. Baste rickrack to mane; baste mane to body; applique mane to body with invisible hand stitches.

11. Quilting and embroidery are done together, by passing the needle through all layers to the back of the placemat. Blanket-stitch back leg line, using three strands of black embroidery thread. Blanket-stitch mane to body and face to mane. Blanket-stitch nose, cheeks and inner ears. (Blanket-stitch edge of black nose piece where it overlaps white, but do not quilt.)

12. Chain-stitch paw lines (do this on back of mat—paw folds to front). Fold paw to make pocket; pin. Blanket-stitch along folded edge, along bottom and around curved edge of paw, stitching through all layers. Blanket-stitch top of paw, leaving pocket open.

13. Finish all outer edges of mat with blanket stitches.

14. Hem napkin.

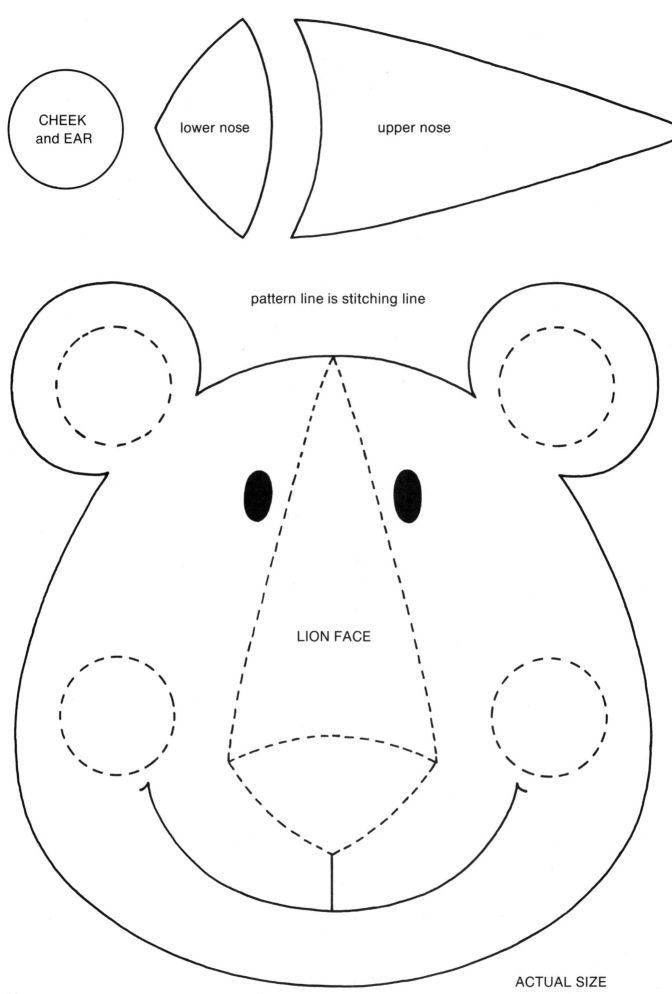

CHEEK and EAR

lower nose

upper nose

pattern line is stitching line

LION FACE

ACTUAL SIZE

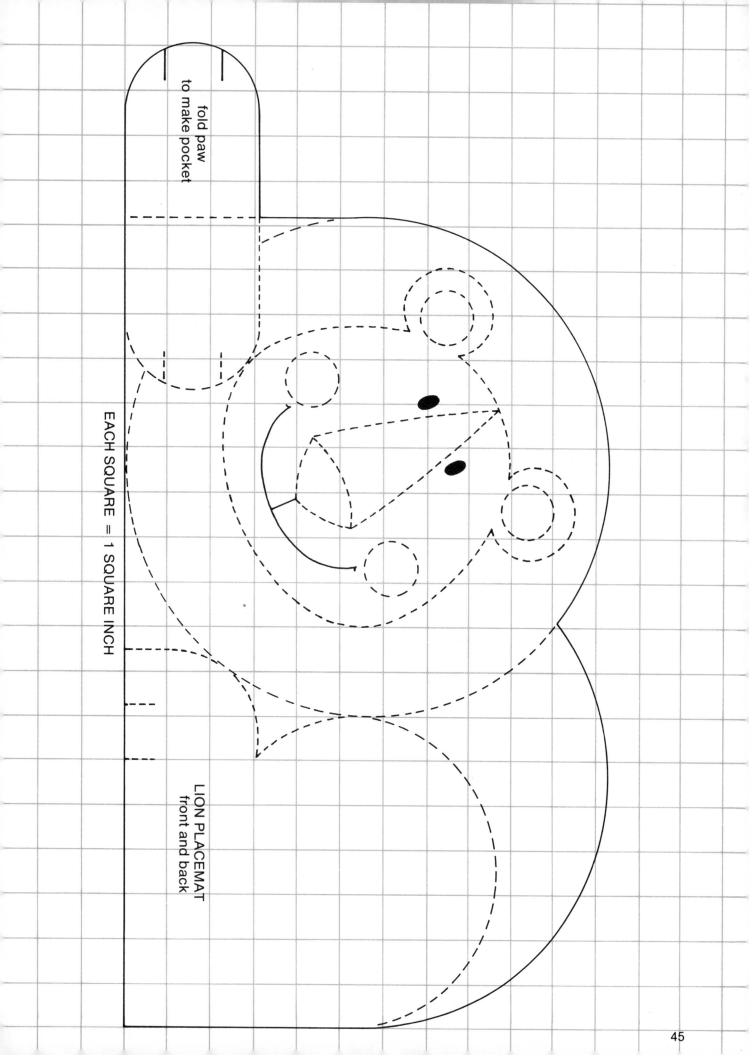

fold paw
to make pocket

EACH SQUARE = 1 SQUARE INCH

LION PLACEMAT
front and back

For the picture, I stuffed GIANT toys. Follow directions for enlarging patterns and you'll have kites and cones two feet long. The wrist watch is so big you can buckle it around a child's waist.

But you could make smaller versions of the scissors, kite, cone and car. Trace the patterns as they are, without enlarging them. Displayed in a bazaar booth, the scissors would make an eye-catching jumbo pincushion. The car might be a potholder if you line it instead of stuffing it. And you might put a zipper in the side of a small cone and sell it as a cosmetic bag. (Note that some of the watch parts are actual size; pattern would have to be reduced to make a small watch.)

PILLOW TOYS

cone

MATERIALS

Pink polka dot scrap, 10x32''
Green polka dot scrap, 9½x35''
⅝ yard brown and white gingham check (45'' wide)
Polyester stuffing

DIRECTIONS

1. Enlarge pattern pieces on tracing paper, following directions in How-to Section; cut out. *Pattern lines are stitching lines.*

2. Trace complete pattern for top scoop on wrong side of pink fabric; bottom scoop on green fabric. Cut two of each, adding ¼'' seam allowance all around. Stitch each scoop (right sides together), leaving a 4'' opening. Trim seams; clip curves; cut into V-areas. Turn right side out and stuff lightly; close opening by hand.

3. Place cone pattern on brown checked fabric so that squares will run diagonally (like a real sugar cone). Trace complete pattern on wrong side of fabric; cut two, adding ¼'' seam allowance. Stitch cone (right sides together), leaving a 5'' opening. Trim seams; clip curves; cut into V-areas. Turn right side out and stuff firmly; close opening by hand.

4. Pin lower scoop to cone. Hand stitch along top curve. Tack on lower scallops. Pin upper scoop to cone, overlapping lower scoop. Hand stitch on back along top curve. Tack to lower scoop.

kite

MATERIALS

Aqua blue fabric, 19x32''
Aqua blue gingham, 18x17''
Brown bias tape, single fold, 44''
1 yard cord
Polyester stuffing

DIRECTIONS

If you want a patchwork-looking kite, cut triangles from four (or eight) different fabrics.

1. Enlarge pattern pieces on tracing paper, following directions in How-to Section; cut out. *Pattern lines are stitching lines.*

2. From aqua blue fabric, cut one complete kite (for back of pillow), adding ¼'' seam allowance all around.

3. Lay check fabric over plain, right sides together; trace one large and one small triangle. Cut out, adding ¼'' seam allowance all around (you'll have one check and one plain triangle in each size.)

4. Join the four triangles to make kite front; stitch; press seams open. Baste bias tape over seams; topstitch.

5. Join kite front to back, right sides together. Machine stitch, leaving 4'' opening on one side, at tail point. Turn right side out. Insert tail cord, secure by hand. Stuff pillow. Close opening with invisible hand stitches.

6. To make tail, cut four pieces of fabric, 6½'' square. Fold right sides together; stitch, leaving 1½'' opening. Turn right side out; press; close opening. Tie cord in a knot around each tail piece 3'' apart. Knot end of cord.

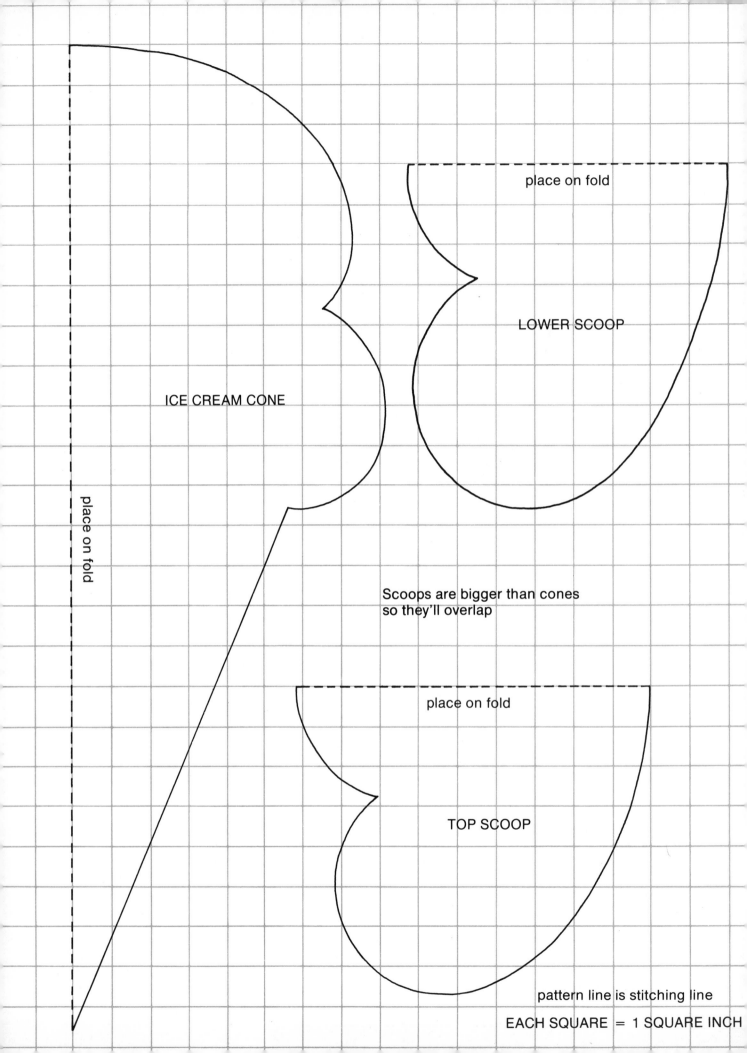

place on fold

LOWER SCOOP

ICE CREAM CONE

place on fold

Scoops are bigger than cones
so they'll overlap

place on fold

TOP SCOOP

pattern line is stitching line

EACH SQUARE = 1 SQUARE INCH

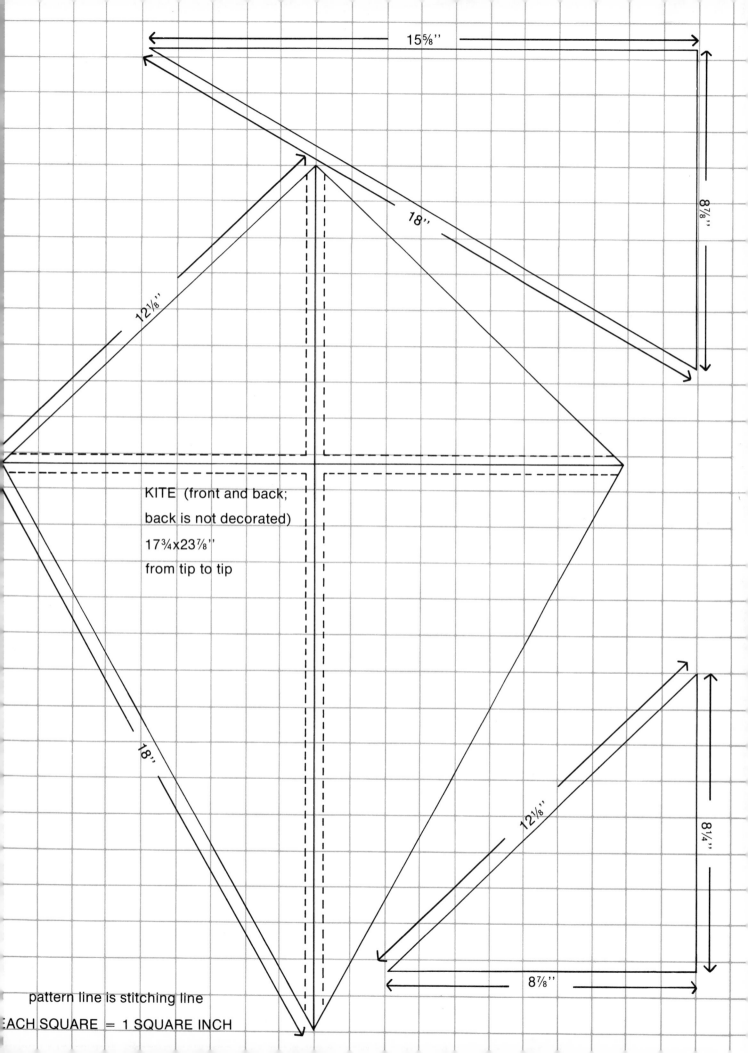

15⅝"

8⅞"

18"

12⅛"

KITE (front and back;
back is not decorated)
17¾x23⅞"
from tip to tip

18"

12⅛"

8¼"

8⅞"

pattern line is stitching line

EACH SQUARE = 1 SQUARE INCH

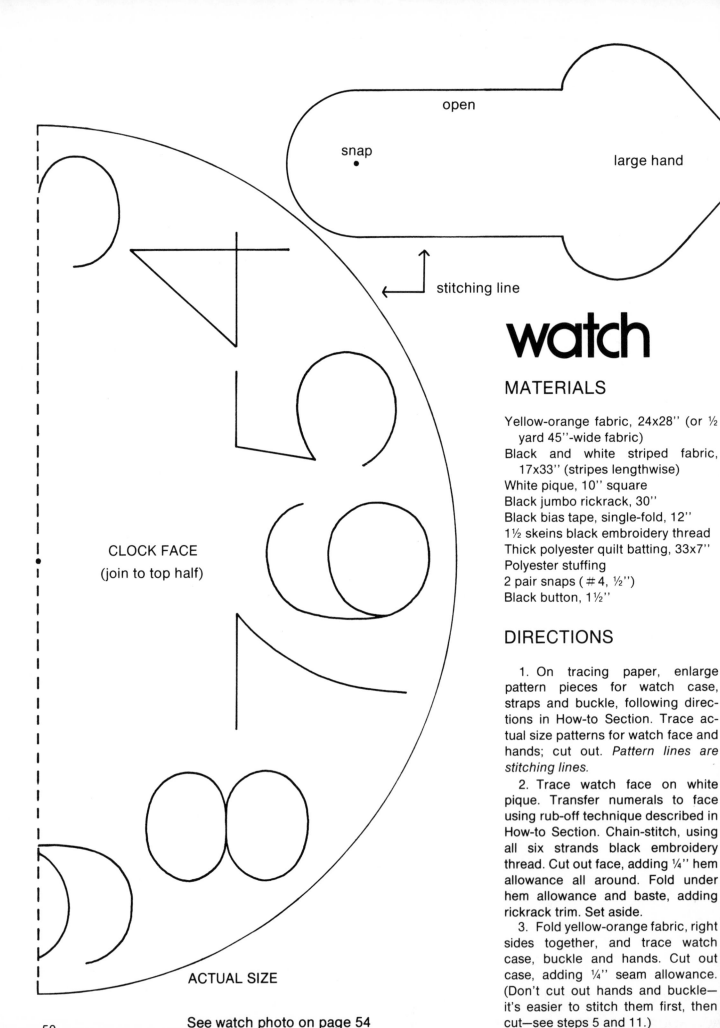

open

snap

large hand

stitching line

CLOCK FACE

(join to top half)

ACTUAL SIZE

watch

MATERIALS

Yellow-orange fabric, 24x28'' (or ½ yard 45''-wide fabric)
Black and white striped fabric, 17x33'' (stripes lengthwise)
White pique, 10'' square
Black jumbo rickrack, 30''
Black bias tape, single-fold, 12''
1½ skeins black embroidery thread
Thick polyester quilt batting, 33x7''
Polyester stuffing
2 pair snaps (# 4, ½'')
Black button, 1½''

DIRECTIONS

1. On tracing paper, enlarge pattern pieces for watch case, straps and buckle, following directions in How-to Section. Trace actual size patterns for watch face and hands; cut out. *Pattern lines are stitching lines.*

2. Trace watch face on white pique. Transfer numerals to face using rub-off technique described in How-to Section. Chain-stitch, using all six strands black embroidery thread. Cut out face, adding ¼'' hem allowance all around. Fold under hem allowance and baste, adding rickrack trim. Set aside.

3. Fold yellow-orange fabric, right sides together, and trace watch case, buckle and hands. Cut out case, adding ¼'' seam allowance. (Don't cut out hands and buckle—it's easier to stitch them first, then cut—see steps 5 and 11.)

See watch photo on page 54

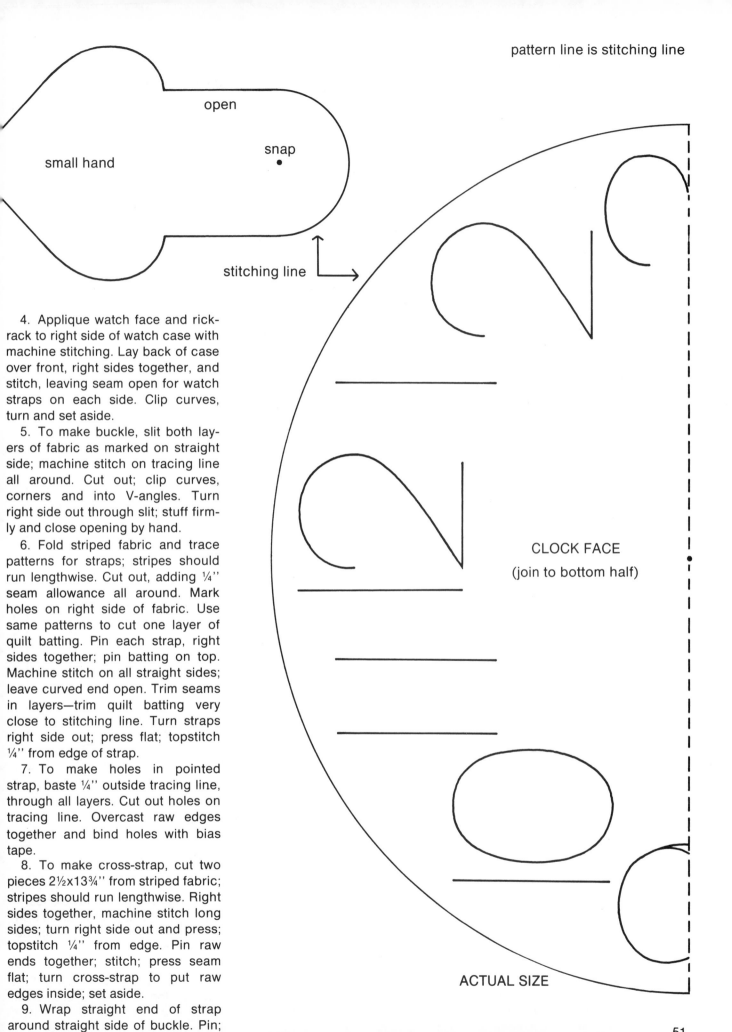

open

small hand

snap
•

stitching line →

4. Applique watch face and rickrack to right side of watch case with machine stitching. Lay back of case over front, right sides together, and stitch, leaving seam open for watch straps on each side. Clip curves, turn and set aside.

5. To make buckle, slit both layers of fabric as marked on straight side; machine stitch on tracing line all around. Cut out; clip curves, corners and into V-angles. Turn right side out through slit; stuff firmly and close opening by hand.

6. Fold striped fabric and trace patterns for straps; stripes should run lengthwise. Cut out, adding ¼'' seam allowance all around. Mark holes on right side of fabric. Use same patterns to cut one layer of quilt batting. Pin each strap, right sides together; pin batting on top. Machine stitch on all straight sides; leave curved end open. Trim seams in layers—trim quilt batting very close to stitching line. Turn straps right side out; press flat; topstitch ¼'' from edge of strap.

7. To make holes in pointed strap, baste ¼'' outside tracing line, through all layers. Cut out holes on tracing line. Overcast raw edges together and bind holes with bias tape.

8. To make cross-strap, cut two pieces 2½x13¾'' from striped fabric; stripes should run lengthwise. Right sides together, machine stitch long sides; turn right side out and press; topstitch ¼'' from edge. Pin raw ends together; stitch; press seam flat; turn cross-strap to put raw edges inside; set aside.

9. Wrap straight end of strap around straight side of buckle. Pin;

CLOCK FACE
(join to bottom half)

ACTUAL SIZE

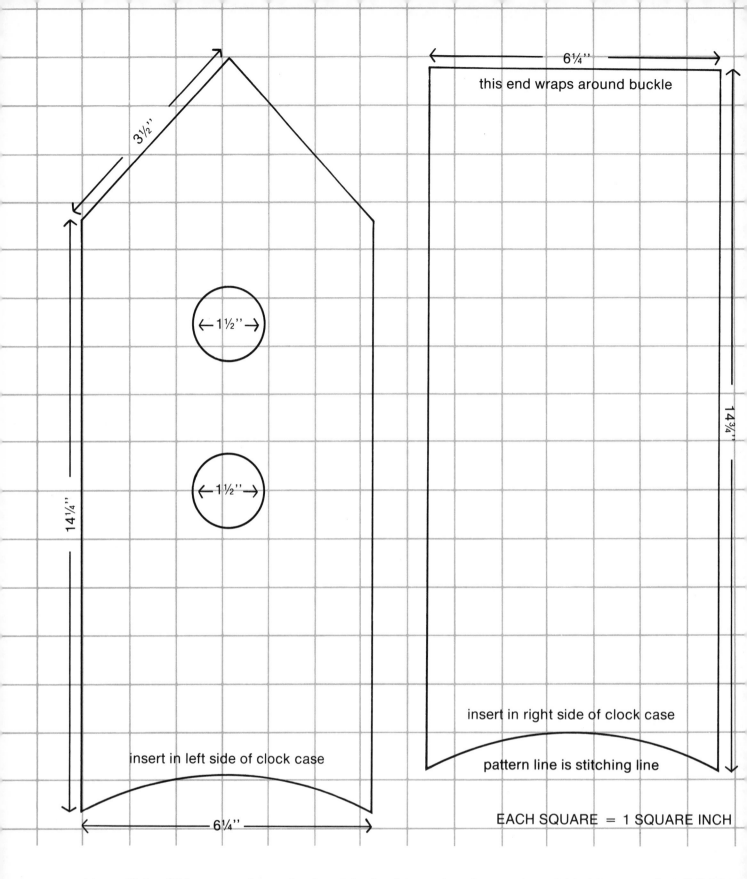

3½''

6¼''

this end wraps around buckle

←1½''→

14¾''

←1½''→

14¼''

insert in right side of clock case

insert in left side of clock case

pattern line is stitching line

6¼''

EACH SQUARE = 1 SQUARE INCH

machine stitch. Slide cross-strap over strap, placing it snug against buckle. Tack cross-strap to strap at back; leave front loose.

10. Now back to the watch case. Turn under seam allowance in seams you left open in step 4; baste. Insert raw edge of strap with buckle into opening on right edge of watch case; pin and hand stitch strap to

front and back of base. Insert raw edge of pointed strap into left opening; pin and sew only to front of watch case. Stuff case very firmly through back opening; close the opening and secure strap with hand stitches.

11. Stitch hands, right sides together, leaving one side open. Cut out, clip curves and into V-angles;

turn right side out and stuff lightly. Close opening with hand stitches.

12. Sew one pair of snaps to front and back of long hand, passing needle through hand to get a "tufted" effect. Sew second pair of snaps to watch face and to small hand. Sew black button to other side of small hand. Snap large hand to watch; snap small hand to large hand.

EACH SQUARE = 1 SQUARE INCH

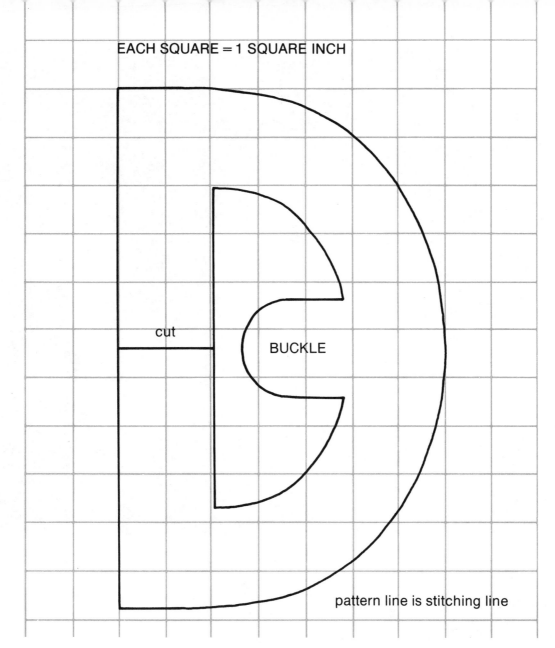

cut

BUCKLE

pattern line is stitching line

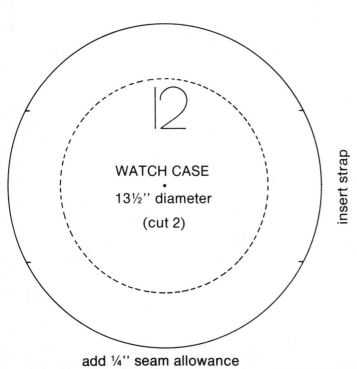

12

WATCH CASE
·
13½'' diameter

(cut 2)

insert strap

add ¼'' seam allowance

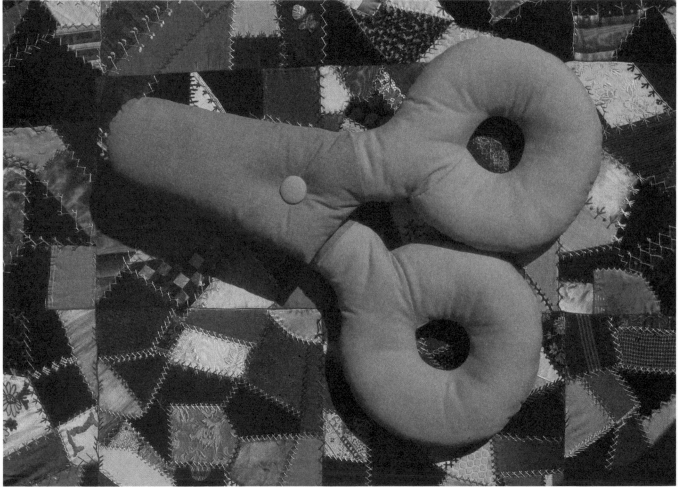

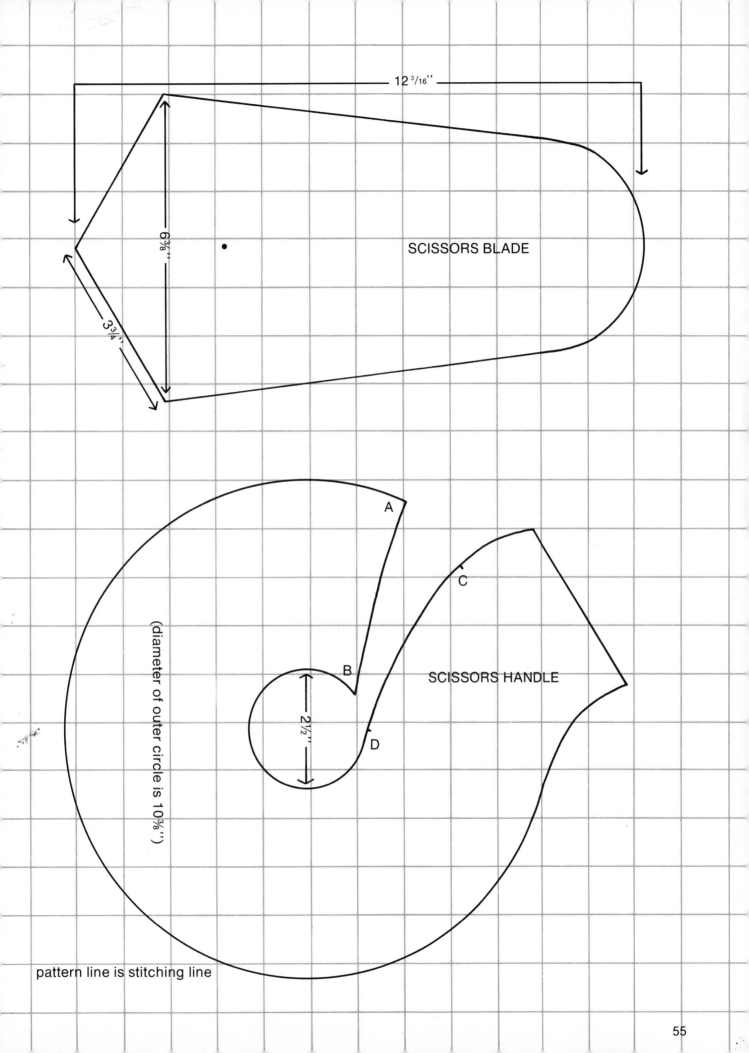

12 3/16''

6 3/8''

3 3/4''

SCISSORS BLADE

A

C

B

(diameter of outer circle is 10 3/8'')

2 1/2''

SCISSORS HANDLE

D

pattern line is stitching line

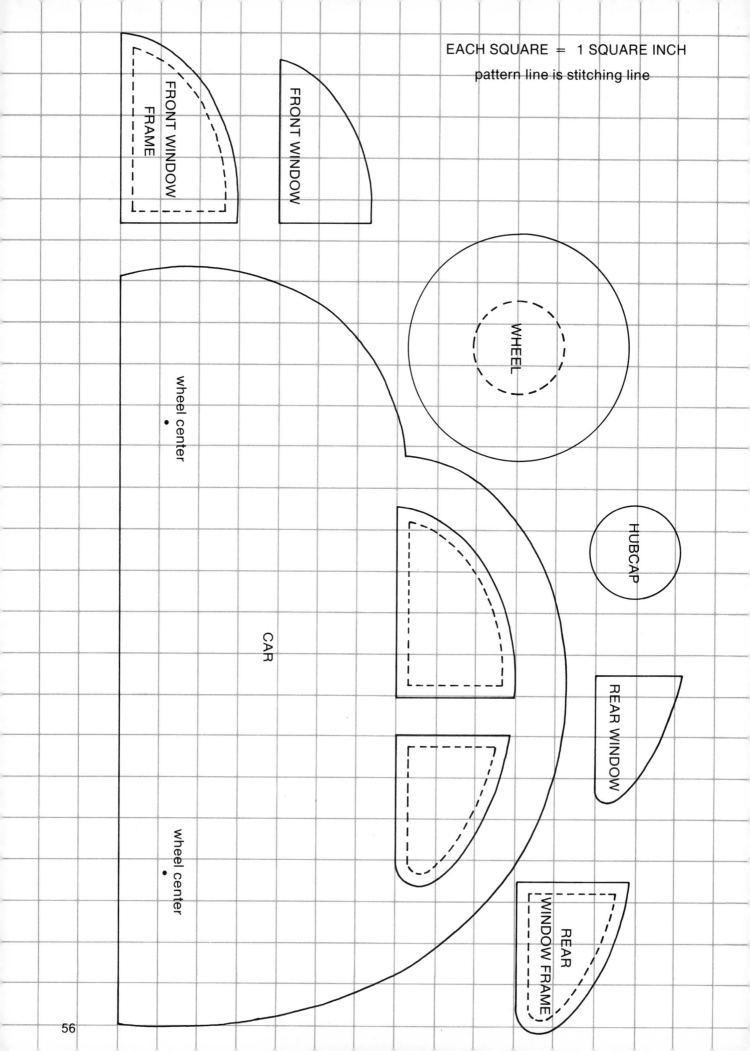

EACH SQUARE = 1 SQUARE INCH

pattern line is stitching line

FRONT WINDOW
FRAME

FRONT WINDOW

WHEEL

wheel center

•

HUBCAP

CAR

REAR WINDOW

wheel center

•

REAR
WINDOW FRAME

56

scissors

MATERIALS

Gray fabric, 13x27''
Lavendar fabric, 13x45''
Polyester stuffing
1 pair snaps (# 4, ½'')
2 buttons (at least 1'')

DIRECTIONS

1. Enlarge pattern pieces on tracing paper, following directions in How-to Section; cut out. *Pattern lines are stitching lines.*

2. Fold gray fabric; cut two pairs of scissors blades, adding ¼'' seam allowance. Mark position for snap and button.

3. Fold lavendar fabric; cut two pairs of scissors handles, adding ¼'' seam allowance.

4. Right sides together, join each of the four handle pieces to a blade

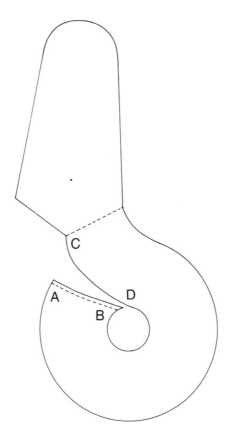

piece—see sketch for seamline. Stitch; press seam open.

5. Right sides together, stitch each pair of scissors together, leaving seam open on handle between A-B and C-D. Clip corners; clip curves; cut into V-angles. Turn right side out and stuff; pillow should be firm, but rather flat.

6. To complete handle, insert end A-B into opening C-D; pin; then hand stitch securely.

7. Sew large snap to inside of both blades using strong double thread. Sew buttons to outside. Pass needle through blade several times at this point, pulling gently, to get "tufted" effect. Snap scissors together.

car

MATERIALS

Red quilted fabric, 24x19½''
Black on white polka dot scrap, 12x3''
White on black polka dot scrap, 12½x24''
White pique scrap, 9x6''
Black scrap, 10x7''

DIRECTIONS

1. Enlarge pattern on tracing paper according to directions in How-to Section; cut out. *Pattern lines are stitching lines.*

2. Fold red fabric, cut two car bodies, adding ¼'' seam allowance all around. Mark positions for windows and wheels on front of fabric.

3. Fold white and black scraps; cut two front and two back windows and window frames, adding ¼'' hem allowance all around. Cut eight wheels from black polka dot scrap, and four hubcaps from white polka

dot scrap, adding ¼'' seam allowance all around.

4. Turn under window and window frame hem allowances; baste windows to frames; baste frames to car. Topstitch around both windows and frames.

5. Pin car pieces, right sides together, and stitch, leaving 4'' opening along bottom edge. Clip curves and into V-angles; turn pillow right side out; stuff; close opening with invisible hand stitches.

6. To make wheel, turn under hem allowance on hubcap; baste hubcap to wheel. Topstitch. Pin wheel front to wheel back, right sides together; stitch, leaving 1½'' opening. Clip curves, turn right side out; stuff; close opening with invisible hand stitches. Repeat to make four wheels.

7. Quilt around hubcaps with double thread, passing needle to back of wheels and pulling thread tight. This shapes tires—makes them look full.

8. Tack wheels to car along top curve.

Giant schools of goldfish swimming to the left and right make the pattern for this shower curtain. The design is worked in panels and entirely machine stitched (even the applique and embroidery), so it's not quite the monumental task it appears to be!

The instructions are for a standard 70x72'' shower curtain; however, the one pictured is 78'' long. I added a few inches top and bottom because I wanted mine to reach the floor.

If you'd rather make a quilt with this pattern, adjust the 70x72'' dimensions to fit your bed by adding or subtracting panels of fish, and by increasing or decreasing the water area at top and bottom. Choose an appropriate fabric for the quilt backing (maybe some big orange polka dots) and place a layer of quilt batting between quilt top and backing. Finish the quilt edges with bias tape or just seam and topstitch them. Stitch around each fish and water section to make the quilt puffy and hold the batting in place.

By cutting checked goldfish on the straight of goods rather than the bias, you can manage with two yards of gingham. But if you like the checks running diagonally, you'll need the three yards specified.

GOLDFISH SHOWER CURTAIN

MATERIALS

4½ yards orange fabric (poplin weight; 45'' wide)
3 yards orange checked gingham (1'' checks)
1¼ yards aqua fabric (poplin weight; 45'' wide)
Pink fabric, 12x18''
Fusible web, 12x18''
White iron-on fabric, 6½x14''
Black iron-on fabric, 7x7''
2 yards buckram, 3''wide
Shower curtain eyelets
Plastic shower curtain liner, 69x72''

DIRECTIONS

Finished shower curtain is approximately 70x72''. All pattern pieces are actual size.

1. Trace fish patterns, head and tail, butting them together on dotted line to make a complete fish. Trace water sections, joining them on dotted lines to make complete waves. Trace separate patterns for eye, pupil and cheek. Rubber cement all patterns to lightweight cardboard and cut out. (Cardboard is essential—you'll be tracing around each pattern fifty times.)

2. With an X-acto knife, cut out eye and cheek circles in fish pattern; also cut eyelash and smile lines, so pattern can be used as a template to mark features on fabric.

3. Cut five panels of orange fabric, each one 15x78½''. (This includes ½'' seam allowance on each side.) Number each panel.

4. Panels 1, 3 and 5 are alike. Measure 8'' from top of panel on left seam line (½'' from edge). Place tail of fish pattern at this point and trace fish—fish faces right. Trace features, using a light pencil line.

5. Flip pattern so fish faces left; match pattern to curves of first fish and complete tracing for second fish. Continue tracing fish down panel in this way (see diagram) until you have ten fish; there should be 8'' left at bottom of panel. Do not trace features on the fish facing left—these will be appliqued with checked fabric.

6. Panels 2 and 4 are alike. Place tail of fish pattern on right seam line, 8'' from top of panel and trace fish facing left. Flip pattern and continue tracing fish the length of panel as in step 5. Do not trace features on fish facing left—these will be appliqued.

7. Trace 25 fish outlines on the right side of checked gingham—all with smile facing left, and all on the bias if you want checks to run diagonally. Add ¼'' seam allowances on curves and ½'' on straight edge of tail. Trace facial features and cut out fish.

8. From pink fabric, cut 50 cheeks (no seam allowance needed). Cut 50 circles from fusible web,

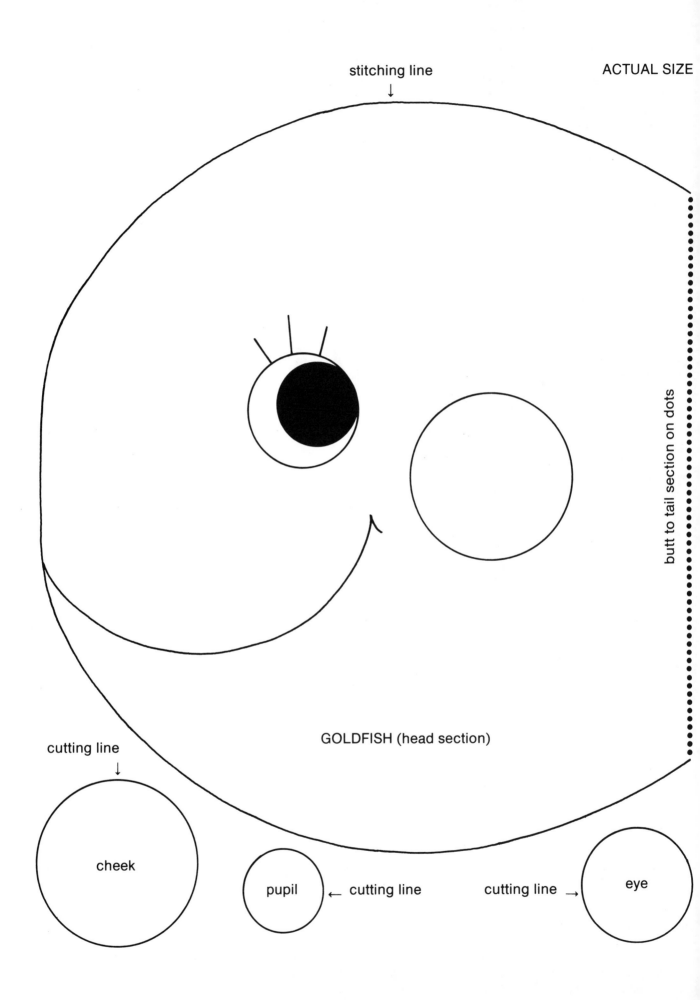

stitching line
↓

ACTUAL SIZE

butt to tail section on dots

GOLDFISH (head section)

cutting line
↓

cheek

pupil ← cutting line

cutting line → eye

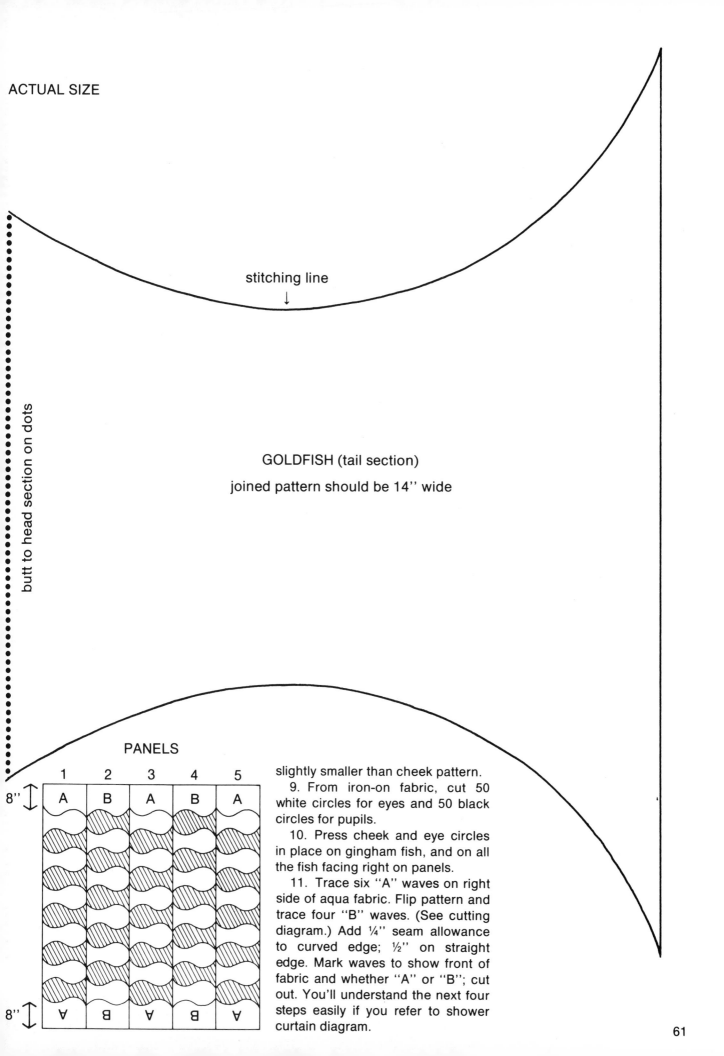

ACTUAL SIZE

butt to head section on dots

stitching line
↓

GOLDFISH (tail section)

joined pattern should be 14" wide

PANELS

1	2	3	4	5
A	B	A	B	A

8"

8"

slightly smaller than cheek pattern.

9. From iron-on fabric, cut 50 white circles for eyes and 50 black circles for pupils.

10. Press cheek and eye circles in place on gingham fish, and on all the fish facing right on panels.

11. Trace six "A" waves on right side of aqua fabric. Flip pattern and trace four "B" waves. (See cutting diagram.) Add ¼" seam allowance to curved edge; ½" on straight edge. Mark waves to show front of fabric and whether "A" or "B"; cut out. You'll understand the next four steps easily if you refer to shower curtain diagram.

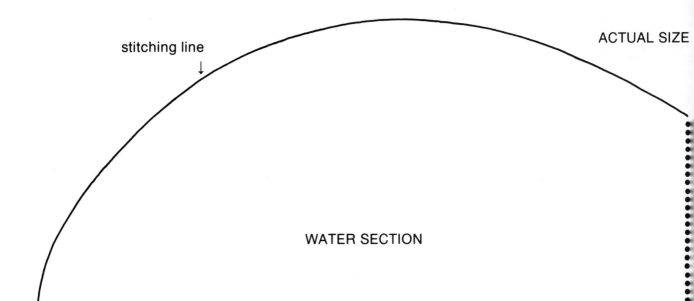

stitching line

↓

ACTUAL SIZE

WATER SECTION

butt to water section on dots

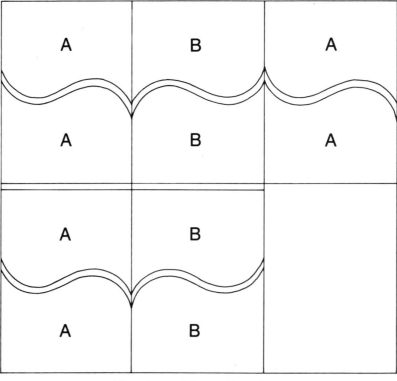

A	B	A
A	B	A
A	B	
A	B	

cutting layout for water pieces

ACTUAL SIZE

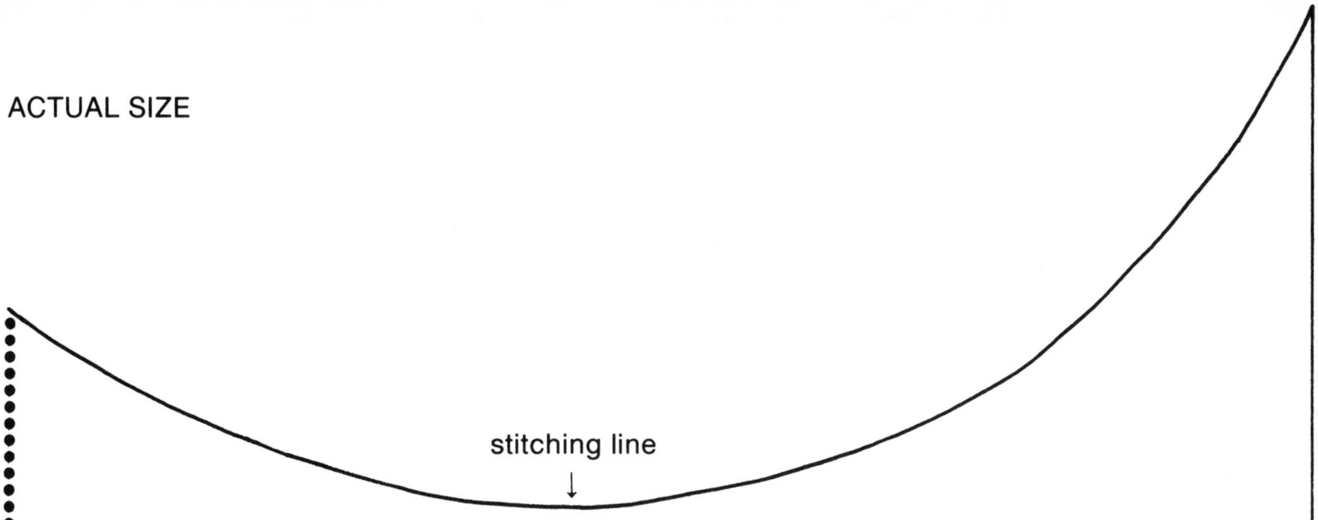

stitching line
↓

WATER SECTION

butt to water section on dots

12. Turn under hem allowance on curved edge of three "A" waves and pin them to tops of panels 1, 3 and 5. Match curved line to tracing of fish curve. Baste along curve; also baste sides within seam allowance.

13. Pin and baste remaining "A" waves to bottoms of panels 1, 3 and 5. Do not turn under hem allowance—applique fish will cover raw edges.

14. Turn under hem allowance on curved edge of two "B" waves and pin to bottoms of panels 2 and 4. Match curved line to tracing of fish. Baste along curve; baste straight sides within seam allowances.

15. Pin and baste remaining "B" waves to tops of panels 2 and 4. Do not turn under hem allowance—applique fish will cover raw edge.

16. Turn under hem allowance on curved edges of checked goldfish; pin and baste them in place on all panels. Topstitch close to edge. Topstitch edge of waves, changing

needle thread to match waves.

17. Embroider fish features by machine, using zigzag stitch. With black thread, applique eyes and pupils; stitch eyelashes. With bright pink thread, applique cheeks; stitch mouth.

18. Pin and stitch panels together and hem sides, using ½" seam allowance. Press seams open.

19. Turn under ¼" at top of curtain. Lay buckram along edge on wrong side and stitch. Turn under top of curtain again to make 3" hem, with buckram interfacing inside. Stitch along top edge.

20. Lay plastic shower curtain liner along top of goldfish shower curtain to mark position for eyelets. Follow directions with eyelet punch to place eyelets.

21. Turn under ¼" at bottom of curtain; stitch. Hang curtain for a few hours before hemming. Turn up hem so that wave area at top and bottom are equal. Hem by hand.

EACH SQUARE =
4 SQUARE INCHES

I wanted this banner to hang outdoors so I planned the design to include some air holes which let the wind pass through. The door window is open and cutout stars are backed with nylon net to hold their edges in line. If you're designing a wall hanging for indoors, you could applique the stars. Use the same plastic suggested for sails so you don't have to turn under hem allowances on star points.

If you have a zigzag attachment on your sewing machine, you might opt to use it instead of turning under hem allowances when you topstitch appliques.

I had some yellow and white fabrics which looked like window panes, but if you substitute plain fabric, you'll find directions for making bias tape window frames.

HOUSE BANNER

MATERIALS

Materials are listed from top to bottom of banner, in order.

SUN AND HEAVENS

Blue polka dot scrap, 24x37''
Yellow scrap for sun aureole, 24x37'' (also used for flowers)
Ochre floral scrap for sun rays, 11x20''
Ochre scrap for sun face, 7x13''
Pink scrap for cheeks, 3x6½''

RAINBOW

Blue-violet scrap, 11½x37''
Magenta scrap, 12½x37''
Orange scrap, 14½x37''
Yellow-orange scrap, 20x37''

SKY AND HOUSE

Aqua blue and white print, 31x37''
Red check for house and chimneys, 15x16''
Black polka dot scrap for roof, 6½x16½''
White scrap for door arch, 5½x9''
Blue scrap for door, 2½x4¼''
Print scrap for door fan, 2½x4''
Yellow scrap for windows, 5x16''
Floral print for flower centers, 3½x7''
Nylon net to back star cutouts, 9x13''

HILLS

Dark green scrap, 11½x37''
Medium green scrap, 12½x37'' (also used for flowers)
Lime scrap, 14½x37''
Chartreuse scrap, 20x37''

LAKE AND BOATS

Blue denim, 19½x37''
4 print scraps for boats, each 2¼x6''
White plastic for sails, 14x14''
Red plastic for flags, 3x6''

LINING AND TRIMS:

2½ yards muslin
½ yard medium green grosgrain ribbon, ⅝''
White jumbo rickrack, 17''
White double-fold bias tape, 3 yards
2 black flat buttons, ⅞''
1 brass button, ⅝''
4 large metal eyelets
1 yard magenta yarn

DIRECTIONS

Finished banner is 3x7'. There are actual-size patterns for many of the details, and a diagram one-eighth actual size to show how pieces fit together. Each square = 4 square inches. The lake, hills and rainbow

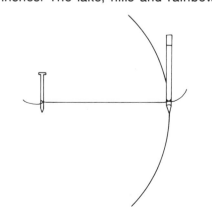

curves are all established from a semicircle 36'' in diameter. Here's how to draw them full size:

1. Make a string compass. Tie a pencil to one end of a 36'' length of string. Make a slip knot 18'' from pencil and tighten it around a nail. Hold nail on the edge of a large piece of brown paper (30x36'') and draw a half-circle with an 18'' radius (that is, 36'' in diameter). This is the pattern for the lake. The first hill is a curve 3'' beyond the edge of the lake curve. Change length of string compass from 18'' to 21''; hold nail at same spot and draw the second arc. Repeat for remaining three arcs, adding 3'' to string length each time—string compass will be 24'', 27'' and 30'' long. Cut paper on

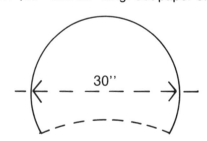

arc lines to get patterns for lake and for each hill. Use hill patterns to cut fabrics for the rainbow—patterns are identical.

2. Shorten string compass to a radius of 15'' and draw pattern for sun aureole 30'' in diameter. Refer to diagram to see how pencil line should go beyond diameter line by approximately 6''. Cut out pattern.

3. On tracing paper, trace actual-size patterns for appliques; cut out patterns. (Note that some patterns

are given as half-patterns, to be laid on folded fabrics for cutting.)

4. Cut lake, hills and rainbow arcs adding hem and seam allowances, ¼" on curves, ½" on each side and 1½" on bottom of lake.

5. Use lake pattern to cut sky, extending sides down 13"; add seam allowances, ¼" on curve, ½" on sides.

6. Cut rectangle for house 11¼x14"; cut two chimneys 3¼x3¾"; cut four windows 2⅜x3¼" and one window 1⅜x2⅜". (House dimensions include seam allowance. Add ¼" seam allowance to windows if you do not bind them—see step 11.)

7. Lay remaining patterns for appliques on designated fabrics, trace and cut out sun face, two cheeks, five rays, one roof, two flowers (including flower centers), six leaves, four boats, four sails and four flags.

8. Hem muslin backing to finished size, 3x7'. Make deep hems at top and bottom, to support eyelets. Set aside.

9. The details are appliqued on sun face, house, sky and lake first; then the major pieces of banner are stitched to banner lining. Turn under and baste hem allowances on all edges that will be appliqued—that is, stitched down. Leave flat all the lower edges that will be overlapped by another applique—this will avoid too much bulkiness under edges. Detailed directions follow.

10. To make sun area: Turn under hem allowance on outer curve of sun aureole; baste. Applique rays to aureole, spacing them accurately. Applique sun face, overlapping sun rays by ¼". Applique cheeks to face. Chain-stitch mouth with magenta yarn.

11. To make house: Stitch double-fold white bias tape to windows to make window panes (see pattern for placement). Bind raw edges of window with tape, mitering corners. Pin to house; stitch. Applique door fan and door to arched white door frame; applique frame to house.

12. Turn under hem allowance on all edges of roof. Pin roof to house, inserting white rickrack trim along lower edge; baste.

13. Turn under hem allowance on top curve of aqua blue sky; baste. Pin house and roof to sky placing top edge of roof 8½" from top edge of sky (see diagram). Pin chimneys in place under edge of roof; machine stitch complete house outline to sky, changing needle thread to match fabric.

14. Pin flower parts in place; applique leaves first, then grosgrain stems each 7½" long. Stitch flower centers to flowers and applique flowers to sky. Set sky piece aside.

15. Turn under hem allowance on boats and applique to blue denim lake. Hold plastic sails and flags in place with transparent tape while you machine stitch close to edge.

16. To assemble banner: Pin and baste blue polka dot heaven to muslin backing, turning under 1" seam allowance on upper edge, and ½" on sides. Pin and baste assembled sun area to heavens.

17. Pin blue-violet rainbow to overlap edge of sun and heavens by ¼". Pin and baste remaining rainbow bands in sequence: magenta, orange and gold, overlapping ¼". Turn under ½" side hems.

18. Pin and baste sky/house area, then green hills shading from dark green to light green, then lake, overlapping each applique ¼" and turning under ½" side hems. At bottom of lake, turn under hem even with lining.

19. For easiest machine stitching, roll banner up tightly and hold together with safety pins, if necessary. Beginning at top, unroll banner to topstitch each applique in place, stitching sides too, and changing needle thread as necessary to match fabric. Continue to bottom, unrolling and rolling banner like a scroll to expose stitching area.

20. To make stars: Trace star pattern on sky five times. Baste outlines, then stitch by machine using closely spaced zigzag stitch. Cut away negative areas. Cut five squares of nylon net 4x4"; place net behind each star opening and machine stitch on star outlines.

21. To make opening in door: Machine stitch ⅛" outside square outline; cut away negative area on outline. Bind raw edges with white bias tape, mitering corners.

22. Sew brass button on door. Sew black button eyes on sun face.

23. Put in eyelets in all four corners.

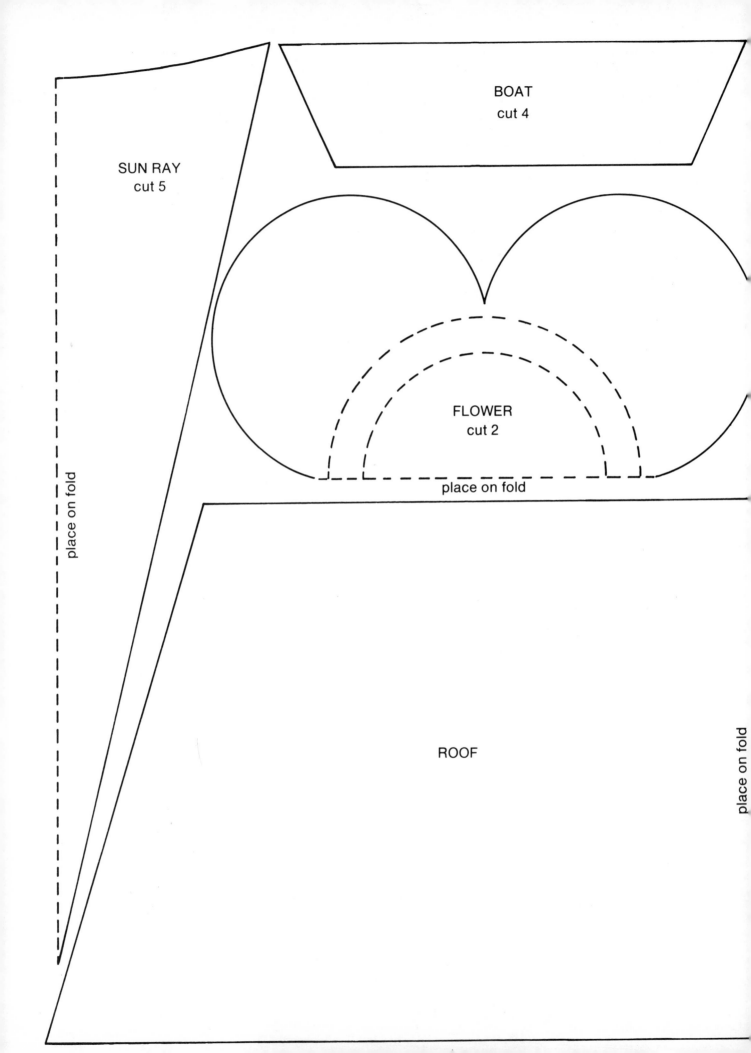

BOAT
cut 4

SUN RAY
cut 5

place on fold

FLOWER
cut 2

place on fold

ROOF

place on fold

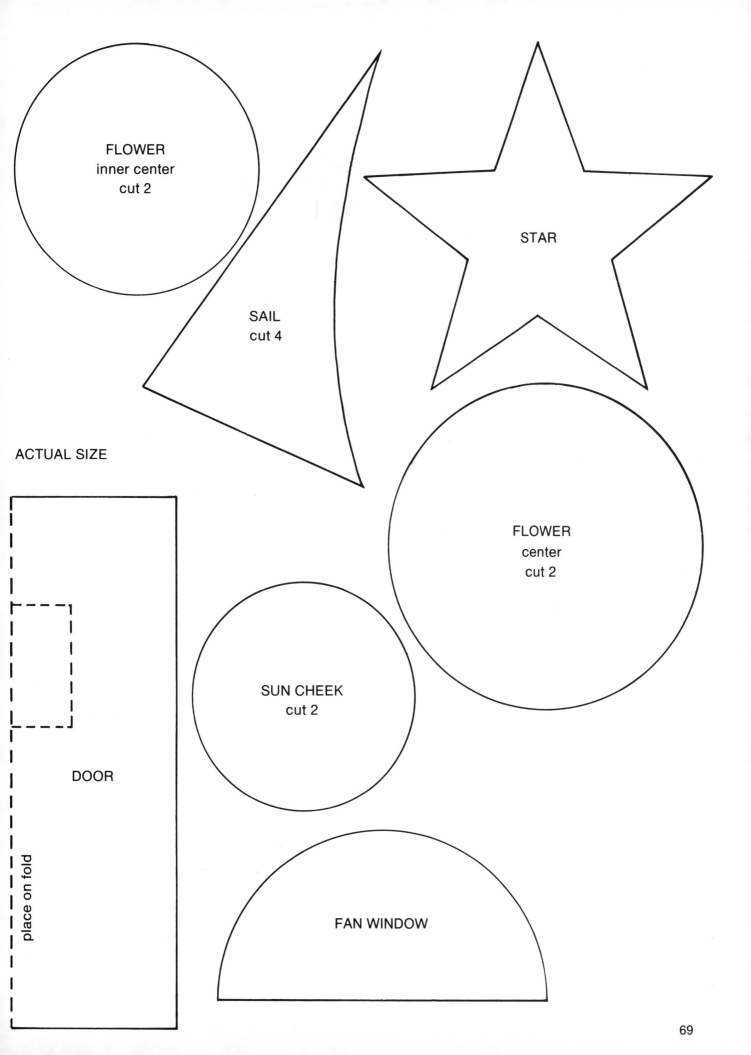

FLOWER
inner center
cut 2

SAIL
cut 4

STAR

FLOWER
center
cut 2

ACTUAL SIZE

SUN CHEEK
cut 2

DOOR

place on fold

FAN WINDOW

69

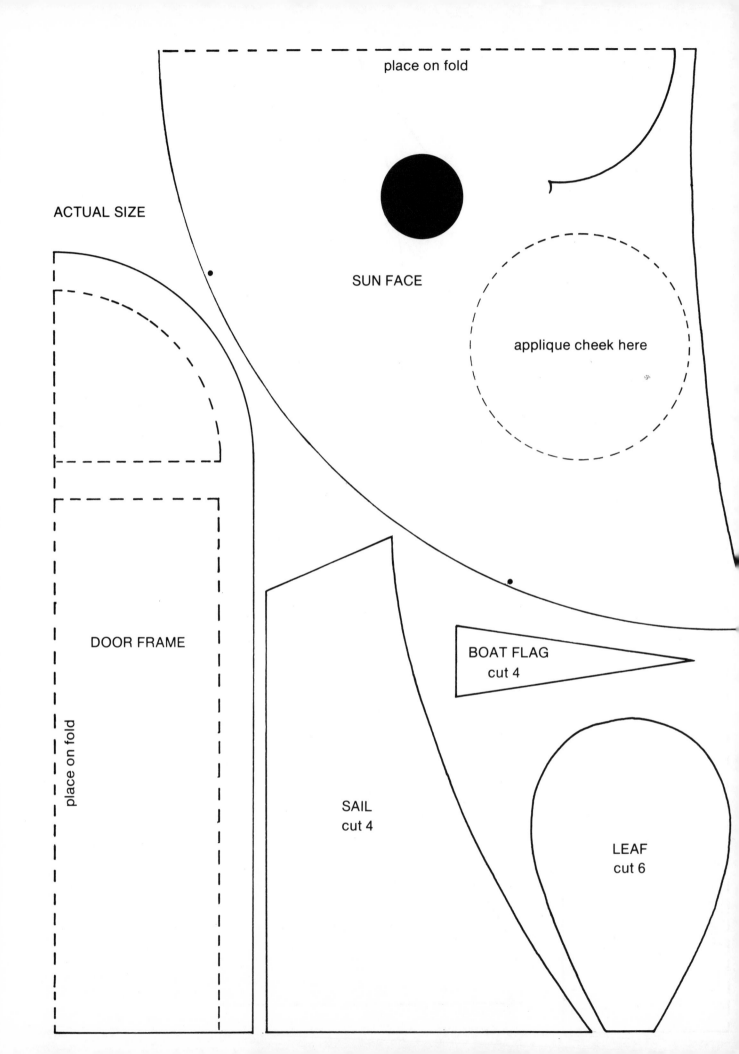

place on fold

ACTUAL SIZE

SUN FACE

applique cheek here

DOOR FRAME

place on fold

BOAT FLAG
cut 4

SAIL
cut 4

LEAF
cut 6

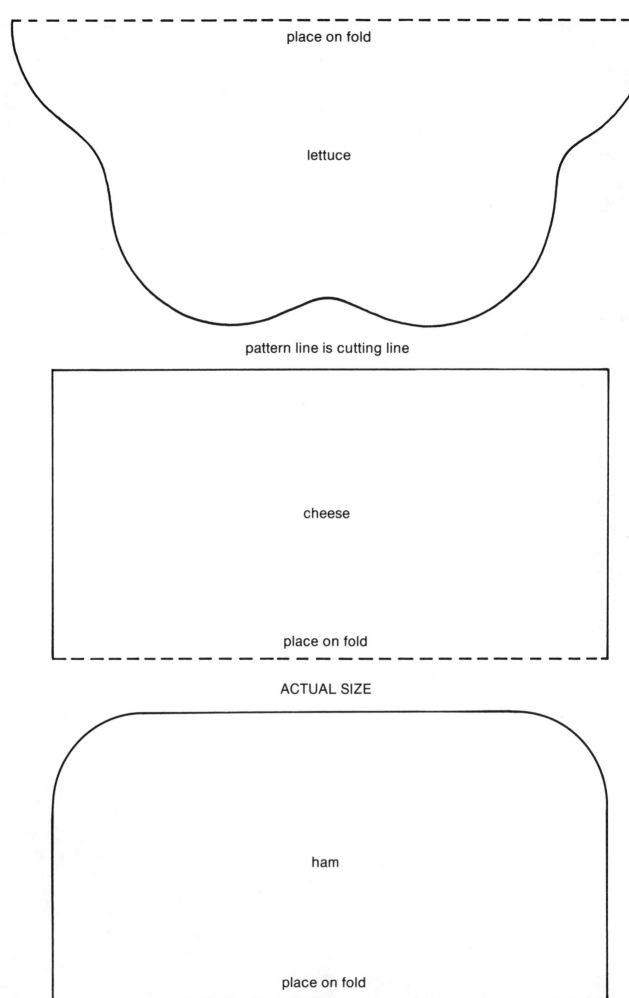

place on fold

lettuce

pattern line is cutting line

cheese

place on fold

ACTUAL SIZE

ham

place on fold

When you make this potholder set for a gift or bazaar sale, package it in a jumbo sandwich bag, closed with a twist-tie. You can add your favorite sandwich makings—slices of purple-edged onion or red tomato. Or make a ten-slice loaf of bread—with brown crusts at each end.

After machine stitching padded layers, you finish the edges with bias tape. It's easiest to do this by hand, and since the holders are small, they make a good take-along project when you're sitting in waiting rooms.

SANDWICH POTHOLDERS

MATERIALS

White textured scrap (terry cloth or pique) 7x13'' for *each* slice bread
Brown wide bias tape, 27'' for *each* slice bread
Green textured scrap (seersucker) for lettuce, 7x15''
Green wide bias tape, 24''
Yellow scrap for cheese, 6½x13''
Yellow wide bias tape, 26''
Pink scrap for ham, 6½x13''
White wide bias tape, 26''
Thick polyester quilt batting, two pieces 6½x6½''; two pieces 7x7''; one piece 7½x7½''
White grosgrain ribbon (or double-fold bias tape), for loops, 15''

DIRECTIONS

1. Patterns are actual size—copy them on folded tracing paper and cut out complete pattern. Pin patterns to folded fabrics; cut out front and back pieces; do not add seam allowance.

2. Using cutout fabrics as guide, cut polyester batting to fit each potholder. Place batting between layers of fabric; fabric is right side out. Pin and baste; remove pins.

3. Fold 3'' length of ribbon or bias tape to make loop; sew ends to top center edge of each potholder. (Loop lays down flat against potholder.)

4. Machine stitch all around each potholder ⅜'' from edge, using large stitches. Trim away excess batting.

5. Fold and press wide bias tape to ½'' width and hand stitch around edges of each potholder.

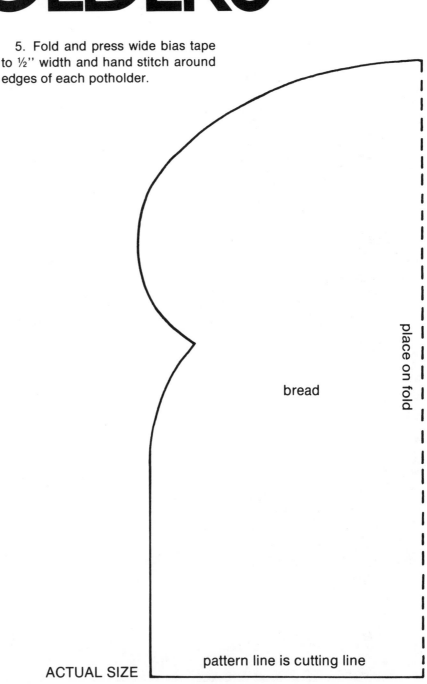

bread

place on fold

ACTUAL SIZE

pattern line is cutting line

Even when it's raining outside, you can start your day with a ray of sunshine if you stitch up these placemats. They go together quickly because you join the sections and do quilting on your sewing machine.

If you use a striped scrap for some of the sun's rays, center the stripes each time you trace the pattern for a neater look. Cut checked fabrics on the bias or the straight of goods—either way looks good.

If your scrap basket seems to be full of flower colors, cut petals instead of sun rays. You could round the pointed end on the pattern.

Another way to use this pattern is to enlarge it (directions in the How-to Section), making one huge sun, big enough to cover your table top. If you feel ambitious, you could also make small suns for coasters.

SUNSHINE PLACEMATS

MATERIALS

For two placemats, two napkins:

1 yard yellow fabric (45'' wide)
¼ yard each of 4 different yellow and orange fabrics (or 4 scraps, 14x14''—solids or prints)
Light orange scrap, 5x5''
Black and red-orange embroidery thread
Polyester quilt batting, 19x37''

DIRECTIONS

1. Trace actual-size patterns and cut them out. Make pattern for backing piece by tracing sun circle on 19'' square paper. Mark dots around perimeter, trace sun rays between dots to complete pattern (see diagram). *Pattern lines are stitching lines.*

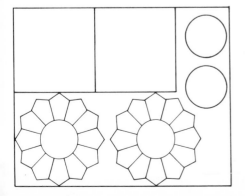

2. On wrong side of yellow fabric, trace pattern outlines for two backing pieces and two sun centers; cut out, adding ¼'' seam allowance. Also cut two napkins, 17'' square. Transfer details for sun face embroidery (see directions in How-to Section) and mark dots in seam allowance.

3. Trace ray pattern on the wrong side of yellow and orange prints—six rays on each of the four prints. Cut out, adding ¼'' seam allowance.

4. Arrange two rings of twelve rays each, distributing prints in sequence. Right sides together, pin side seams; stitch; remove pins; press seams open.

5. Embroider sun face. Chain-stitch eyes and straight stitch eyebrows, using two strands black thread. Chain-stitch mouth using three strands red-orange thread. (See embroidery stitches in How-to Section.)

6. Cut cheeks from light orange fabric, adding ¼'' hem allowance. Turn under hem; baste; pin cheeks to face. Applique with invisible hand stitches.

7. Right sides together, pin ring of rays to sun face, matching dots and seams. Baste, easing in fullness; stitch. Clip circle curve and press seam toward center.

8. Use backing pattern to cut quilt batting.

9. Layer pieces in this order: batting; backing (right side up); sun face and rays (wrong side up). Carefully line up edges and pin. Machine stitch ¼'' from edge (follow line drawn on rays). Leave one ray unstitched for turning. Clip into V-areas and clip off ray points; trim batting close to stitching line.

10. Turn placemat right side out; close opening with hand stitches. Pin all around outside edge to position seam line exactly on edges; also pin around center to keep batting in place while you quilt.

11. Quilt placemat around sun face and on seams between rays—by hand or machine stitching. Remove pins.

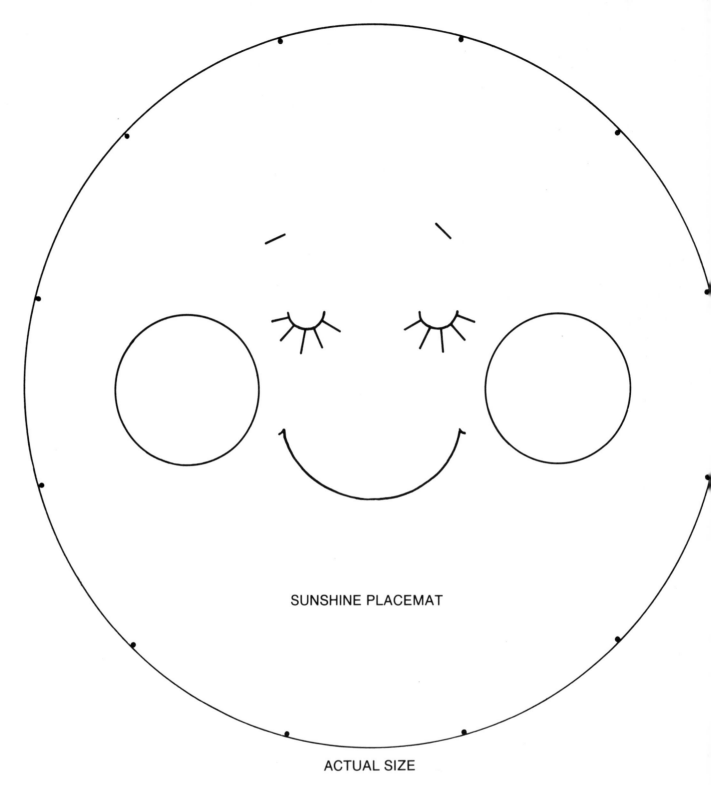

SUNSHINE PLACEMAT

ACTUAL SIZE

pattern lines are stitching lines
add ¼'' seam allowance all around

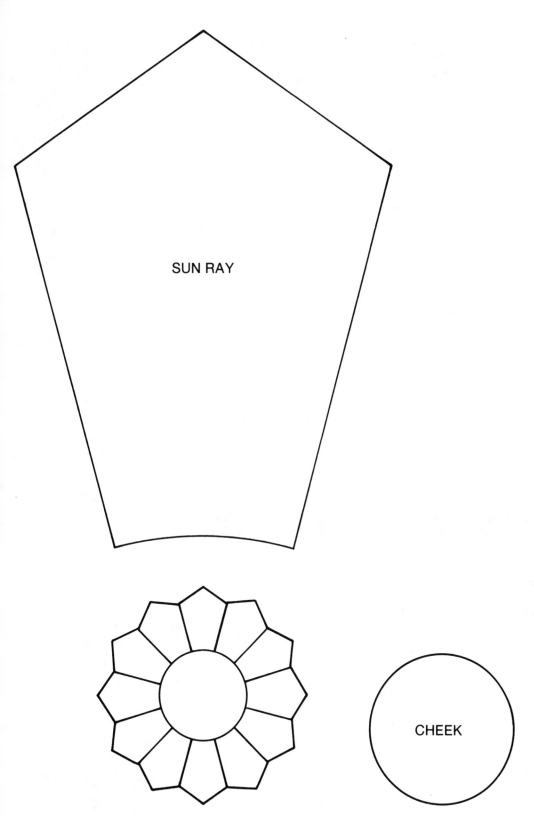

SUN RAY

CHEEK

diagram for completed backing pattern

The figures in this Nativity scene are finished as separate ornaments, so you can move them into the stable one year, or hang them on your tree the next. The Baby tucks into the manger pocket, and the other figures can be tacked to the fabric wall hanging with a few invisible stitches.

There is a good bit of loving stitchery on the little figures. But if you're racing a clock, you can substitute running stitches for blanket stitches. You can even omit the buttonhole stitchery around the edge of cloaks and halos. By choosing bright prints and felts, you'll have a beautiful Nativity scene, even without all the embroidery.

NATIVITY WALL HANGING
nativity figures

GENERAL DIRECTIONS

Patterns for figures are actual size. The outline for fabric bodies is the *stitching line;* the outline for all felt pieces is the *cutting line.*

Wings, hands and halos are cut from double-layer felt. Use a light coat of rubber cement or fusible web to bond two layers of felt together.

Use two strands embroidery thread for all embroidery unless otherwise specified. See How-to Section for stitches and directions for transferring embroidery outlines to fabric.

1. Trace all patterns and cut them out carefully.

2. For each body, fold print fabric right sides together; trace body pattern on wrong side. Do not cut before stitching—it's easier to stitch first, then cut out small figures.

3. Pin the two layers of fabric together and stitch on pencil outlines. Leave ends of sleeves open for hands; leave 1'' open at bottom of figure for turning.

4. Cut out figures, leaving ¼'' allowance on sleeve ends; but trim remaining seams ⅛'' from stitching line. Clip into V-areas at neck and under arms; clip corners of skirts.

5. Turn figures right side out and stuff lightly—they should be soft and rather flat. Close opening on skirt with invisible hand stitches.

6. Make double layer of light pink felt from a piece 3x4'' and trace six big hands and two baby hands. Cut out and embroider edges with small pink blanket stitches. Fold under ¼'' seam allowance on end of each sleeve; insert hand and sew hand to sleeve on front and back with invisible hand stitches.

7. Trace all faces on one scrap of light pink felt 4x4'' and transfer embroidery details. It's easier to embroider faces before you cut them out. Satin-stitch black eyes; backstitch Baby's closed eyes. Satin-stitch medium pink cheeks on angel and Mary; light pink cheeks on Joseph and Baby. With a single strand of embroidery thread, backstitch magenta smiles on angel and Mary; dark pink smiles on Joseph and Baby. Cut out faces.

Specific directions for completing each figure are as follows:

angel

MATERIALS

Brown floral print scrap, 8x5''
Bright orange felt, 3x4''
Yellow felt, 10x6''
Light pink felt as listed in general
    directions
Green felt, 3½x5''
Narrow lace edging, 14''
Embroidery thread: orange, green,
    light pink, medium pink, magenta,
    black
Polyester stuffing
Plastic curtain ring, ¾'' diameter

DIRECTIONS

1. Trace angel body on brown print; sew; stuff; attach hands and embroider face following general directions for Nativity figures.

2. Shirr lace and tack to sleeves and bottom of skirt. Reserve a tiny piece for collar.

3. Cut jumper front and back from green felt; lay over body and join shoulder and side seams with small green blanket stitches. Trim neckline and bottom edge of jumper with a deep band of buttonhole stitches (3/16'') using three strands green embroidery thread.

4. Cut out embroidered face. Cut hair front and back from orange felt. Glue hair and face together. Lay bangs over forehead; snip hair at side so face overlaps hair—see dotted lines on patterns for placement. Use white glue.

5. Glue face and hair to head area of body, tucking reserved piece of shirred lace under chin before glue dries. Glue back hair to back of head. With orange embroidery thread, blanket-stitch all around edge of hair, including bangs.

6. With light pink thread, embroider blanket stitches around edge of face.

7. Stitch a length of green embroidery thread (all six strands) at each side of head and tie for hairbows. Knot ends to keep them from untwisting.

8. Cut halo and wings from double layer of yellow felt. Trim scalloped edges with buttonhole stitches (3/16'' deep at wide point of scallop) using three strands yellow embroidery thread. Finish straight sides of wings with small blanket stitches.

9. Slipstitch halo to head; pin wings to back, points just touching; slipstitch in place.

10. Cover curtain ring with yellow buttonhole stitches; tack to top of halo.

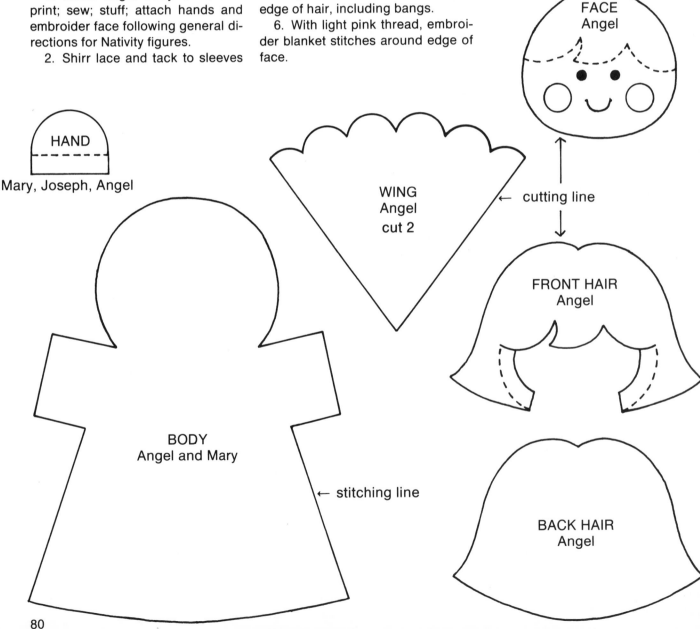

ACTUAL SIZE

FACE
Angel

HAND
Mary, Joseph, Angel

WING
Angel
cut 2

← cutting line

BODY
Angel and Mary

← stitching line

FRONT HAIR
Angel

BACK HAIR
Angel

pattern lines are cutting lines

ACTUAL SIZE

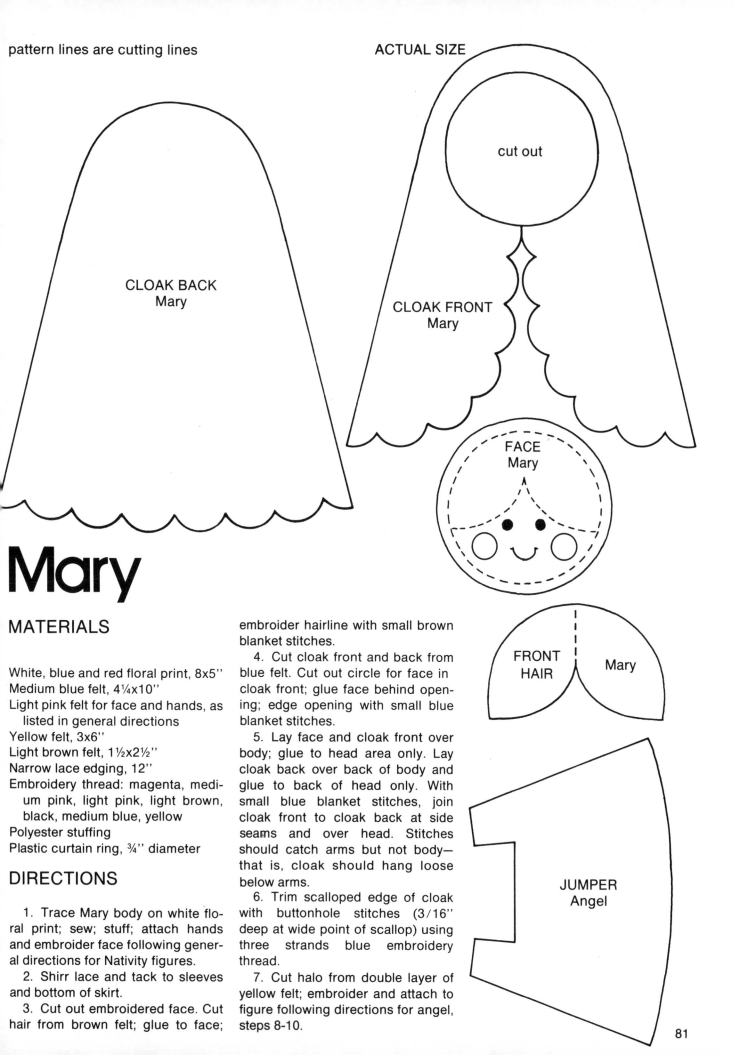

CLOAK BACK
Mary

cut out

CLOAK FRONT
Mary

FACE
Mary

FRONT
HAIR   Mary

Mary

JUMPER
Angel

MATERIALS

White, blue and red floral print, 8x5''
Medium blue felt, 4¼x10''
Light pink felt for face and hands, as
    listed in general directions
Yellow felt, 3x6''
Light brown felt, 1½x2½''
Narrow lace edging, 12''
Embroidery thread: magenta, medi-
    um pink, light pink, light brown,
    black, medium blue, yellow
Polyester stuffing
Plastic curtain ring, ¾'' diameter

DIRECTIONS

1. Trace Mary body on white floral print; sew; stuff; attach hands
and embroider face following general directions for Nativity figures.

2. Shirr lace and tack to sleeves
and bottom of skirt.

3. Cut out embroidered face. Cut
hair from brown felt; glue to face;

embroider hairline with small brown
blanket stitches.

4. Cut cloak front and back from
blue felt. Cut out circle for face in
cloak front; glue face behind opening; edge opening with small blue
blanket stitches.

5. Lay face and cloak front over
body; glue to head area only. Lay
cloak back over back of body and
glue to back of head only. With
small blue blanket stitches, join
cloak front to cloak back at side
seams and over head. Stitches
should catch arms but not body—
that is, cloak should hang loose
below arms.

6. Trim scalloped edge of cloak
with buttonhole stitches (3/16''
deep at wide point of scallop) using
three strands blue embroidery
thread.

7. Cut halo from double layer of
yellow felt; embroider and attach to
figure following directions for angel,
steps 8-10.

81

Joseph

MATERIALS

Beige and blue check scrap, 8x5''
Yellow felt, 6x3''
Beige felt, 3⅓x7''
Light brown felt, 3x5''
Medium brown felt, 3x5''
Light pink felt for face and hands, as listed in general directions
Embroidery thread: light pink, dark pink, black, light brown, medium brown, beige or taupe, yellow
Polyester stuffing
Plastic curtain ring, ¾'' diameter

DIRECTIONS

1. Trace Joseph body on check fabric; sew; stuff; attach hands and **embroider face following general directions for Nativity figures.**

2. Braid three pieces of medium brown embroidery thread (use all six strands) to a length of 10'' and tie around Joseph's waist. Adjust length and knot ends to make tassels.

3. From beige felt, cut coat back and two coat fronts (left and right). Pin coat pieces to body. Join shoulder and side seams with small beige blanket stitches. Do not catch body in side seams—cloak should hang loose.

4. Embroider edges of front opening and bottom of cloak and sleeves with wide band of buttonhole stitches (3/16''), using three strands of beige embroidery thread.

5. Cut out embroidered face. From medium brown felt, cut hair and beard, front and back. Glue hair and beard to face; applique hairline to face with medium brown blanket stitches.

6. Glue face and hair to head area of body; glue back hair to back of head. With medium brown thread, blanket-stitch around top of head and on edge of beard. Do not attach beard to body—let it hang loose.

7. Cut staff from double layer of light brown felt; edge with small light brown blanket stitches and tack to back of Joseph's hand.

8. Cut halo from double layer of yellow felt; embroider and attach to figure following directions for angel, steps 8-10.

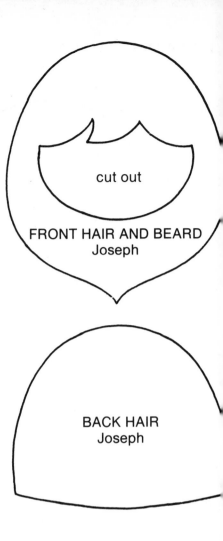

FRONT HAIR AND BEARD
Joseph

cut out

BACK HAIR
Joseph

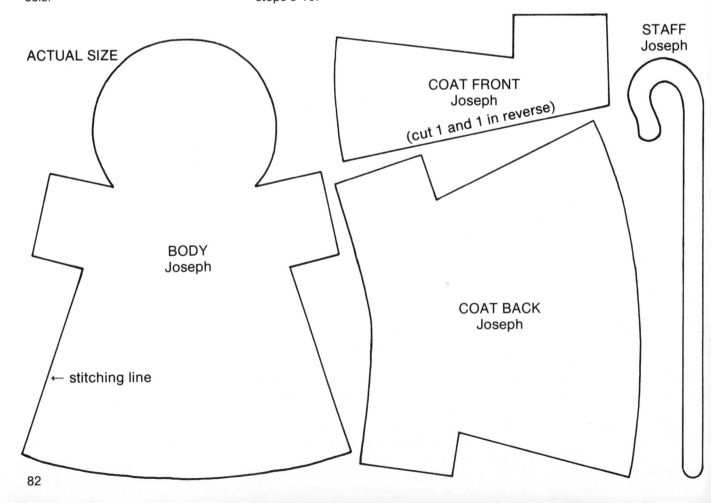

ACTUAL SIZE

BODY
Joseph

← stitching line

COAT FRONT
Joseph
(cut 1 and 1 in reverse)

COAT BACK
Joseph

STAFF
Joseph

baby

MATERIALS

Blue and white small check scrap, 3x6''

Light brown felt, 3x1¼''

Light pink felt for face and hands, as listed in general directions

Yellow felt, 2½x4½''

White felt, 4x4''

Embroidery thread: light brown, black, yellow, light pink, dark pink, blue

Polyester stuffing

Plastic curtain ring, ¾'' diameter

DIRECTIONS

1. Trace Baby body on check fabric; sew; stuff; attach hands and embroider face following general directions for Nativity figures.

2. Cut out embroidered face. Cut hair from light brown felt. Glue hair to face; glue face to head area of body; glue back hair to back of head. With light brown embroidery thread, blanket-stitch all around edge of hair, including bangs.

3. Blanket-stitch around edge of face with light pink thread.

4. Cut halo from double layer of yellow felt; embroider and attach to figure following directions for angel, steps 8-10.

5. Cut baby blanket from white felt; embroider edge with small blue blanket stitches. Lay Baby on blanket, lining up halo on corner "A" (see pattern and diagram for folding). Fold "C" to meet Baby's chin. Bring sides to center; where they meet, sew together ½''. Fold down corners "B" and "D" to uncover Baby's face and body.

stable

MATERIALS

Beige scrap for backing, 20x16''
Green dot or print scrap for grass, 4x13''
Indigo velveteen scrap for interior, 7½x13''
Tan corduroy or other textured scrap for roof, 7x20''
Beige coarse-textured scrap for walls, 7½x10''
Polyester quilt batting, thick, 16x20'' (or two pieces of thin)
Brilliant pink felt, 3x6''
Bright orange felt, 4x4''
Yellow-orange felt, 1½x2½''
Medium green felt, 6x7½''
Light brown felt, 2½x3''
Embroidery thread to match roof, walls, grass and all felt trims
½ yard white scalloped lace (½'')
2 plastic curtain rings, ¾'' diameter.

DIRECTIONS

1. Patterns for stable backing, grass, interior, walls and roof are shown approximately one-quarter size—but they're all straight lines and can be enlarged easily. Use a ruler; draw them on tracing paper to dimensions given. *Pattern line is stitching line.* Cut out patterns; pin to designated fabrics and cut out stable pieces adding ¼'' seam allowance all around each piece.

2. Trace actual-size patterns for manger and flower parts. Pattern tells how many pieces to cut from different felt colors. *Pattern line is cutting line.* Here's a special way to cut flower stem to keep it straight: Make two tracings of pattern, one in reverse. With a light coat of rubber cement, glue uncut patterns to felt; cut out shapes; peel off paper. (Glue sticky side to stable walls in step 8.)

3. To assemble stable: Right sides together, pin grass to interior; stitch and press. Pin walls to each side of interior; stitch and press. Pin roof across top; stitch and press.

4. Use backing pattern to cut out quilt batting. On a flat surface, layer pieces in this order: batting (both layers if you use thin batting); backing (right side up) and stable front (wrong side up). Carefully line up edges and pin. Baste; machine stitch ¼'' from edge, leaving 6'' opening at bottom for turning. Trim batting close to seam; clip corners. Turn stable right side out; close opening with hand stitches.

5. Pin all around outside edge to position seam line exactly on edge. Baste; remove pins. With two strands embroidery thread, blanket-stitch all around edge, matching thread to grass, walls and roof in turn. Or use running stitch instead of blanket stitch.

6. Sew curtain rings to top corners of roof; cover rings with beige embroidery thread, using buttonhole stitches.

7. Quilt stable with small running stitches along seam lines of roof, interior walls and grass. Sew lace trim to lower edge of roof.

8. Use white glue sparingly to attach flower parts to walls. Glue stems first. Lay pink and orange flowers over stem ends; then attach flower centers. Applique stems and flowers to stable walls with blanket stitches, matching the embroidery thread to felt.

9. Glue pink heart to manger; applique with pink blanket stitches. Edge top of manger with light brown blanket stitches. Pin in place at center of stable so that it forms a pocket for Baby. Applique with blanket stitches around sides, across bottom and around legs.

10. Tack Mary and Joseph in place on each side of manger. Tack lower edge of angel skirt to top center of roof. Tuck Baby into manger pocket.

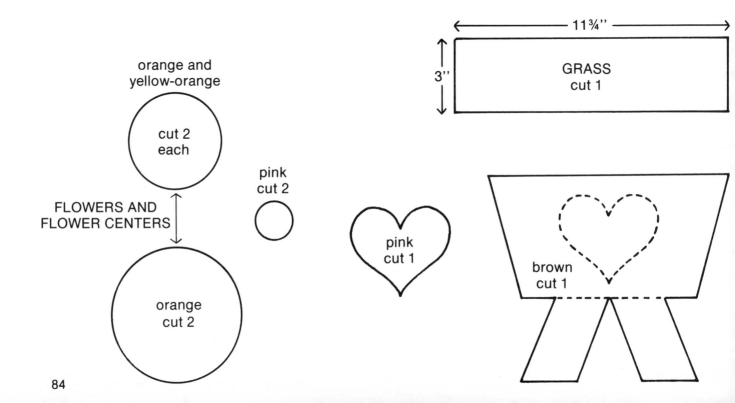

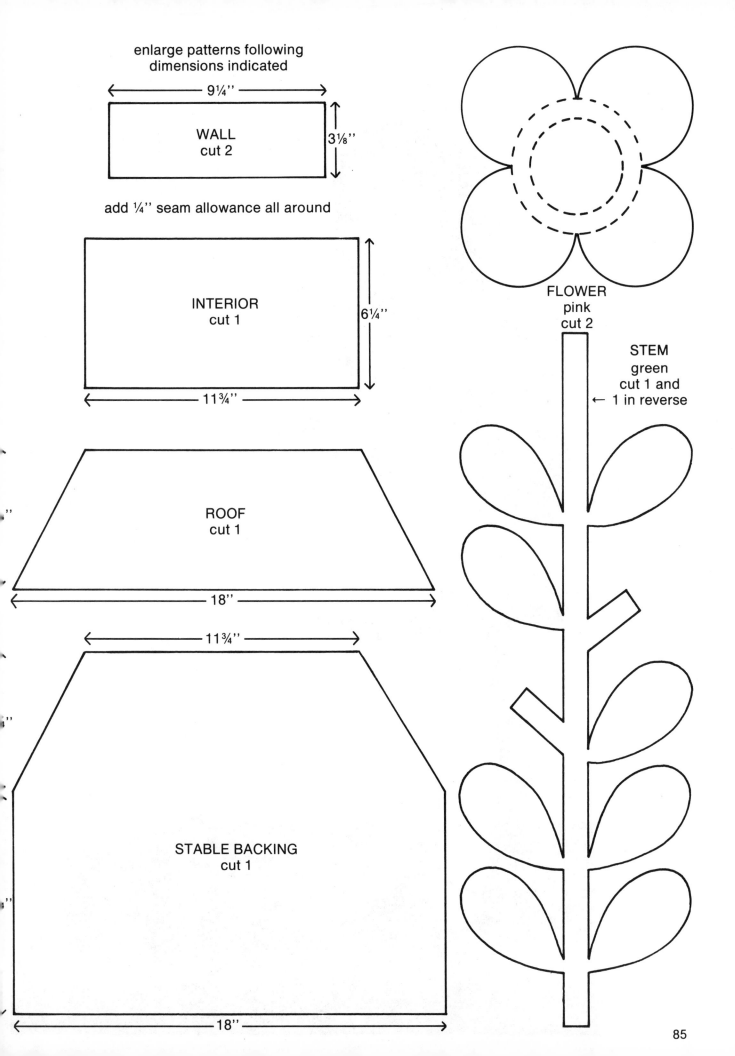

enlarge patterns following
dimensions indicated

9¼''

WALL
cut 2

3⅛''

add ¼'' seam allowance all around

INTERIOR
cut 1

6¼''

11¾''

ROOF
cut 1

18''

11¾''

STABLE BACKING
cut 1

18''

FLOWER
pink
cut 2

STEM
green
cut 1 and
← 1 in reverse

A smiling Santa face is appliqued to the white beard/hatband area on the front of this sandwich board apron. The back is green polka dots, cut from the same pattern outline as the front, and the apron is complete-ly lined with white pique to give it a nice finish and extra strength. If you sew jingle bells to the ends of the ribbon ties, the little person who wears this apron will look like Christmas and sound like it, too!

SANTA APRON

MATERIALS

Green polka dot fabric, 15½x28''
⅝ yard white pique (45'' wide)
Pink scrap, 4x2½''
Red scrap, 8x5''
Pale pink scrap, 5x7''
3¼ yards jumbo white rickrack
1½ yards green ribbon
2 flat black buttons (⅝'')
4 medium-size jingle bells
Medium-size red ball fringe; large white ball fringe
Red embroidery thread

DIRECTIONS

1. On tracing paper, enlarge pattern for apron following directions in How-to Section. Trace actual-size patterns for Santa face, hat and bodice. Cut out patterns.

2. From green polka dot fabric, cut complete apron back plus left and right bodice pieces, adding ¼'' seam allowance all around.

3. Cut hat from red scrap, adding ¼'' seam allowance.

4. From white pique, cut beard/hatband plus two complete apron linings (for front and back), adding ¼'' seam allowance on all pieces.

5. Cut Santa face from pale pink scrap, adding ¼'' hem allowance. Mark positions for features (see transfer directions in How-to Section). Cut two cheeks from pink scrap, adding ¼'' hem allowance. Fold under hem allowance on cheeks; baste cheeks to face. Embroider mouth with chain stitch, using four strands of thread.

6. Fold under and baste hem al-lowance on face; baste face to white beard/hatband. Topstitch cheeks to face and face to beard/hatband.

7. Right sides together, pin green bodice pieces to red hat piece to make bib area of apron; stitch and press seams flat.

8. Fold under seam allowance along top curve of white hatband and baste. Lay white hatband over lower curved edge of bib; pin; baste and topstitch.

9. Turn under shoulder seam al-lowances on linings; press.

10. Right sides together, pin apron front to lining. Stitch all around outside edge and around neck, leaving shoulder seams open for turning. Clip curves and turn right side out. In the same way, sew lining to apron back.

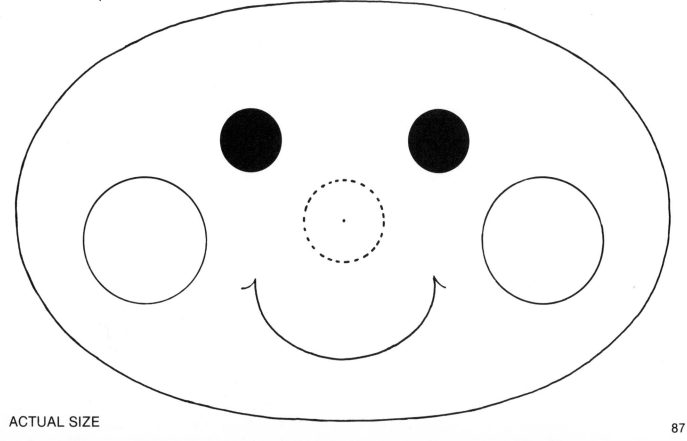

ACTUAL SIZE

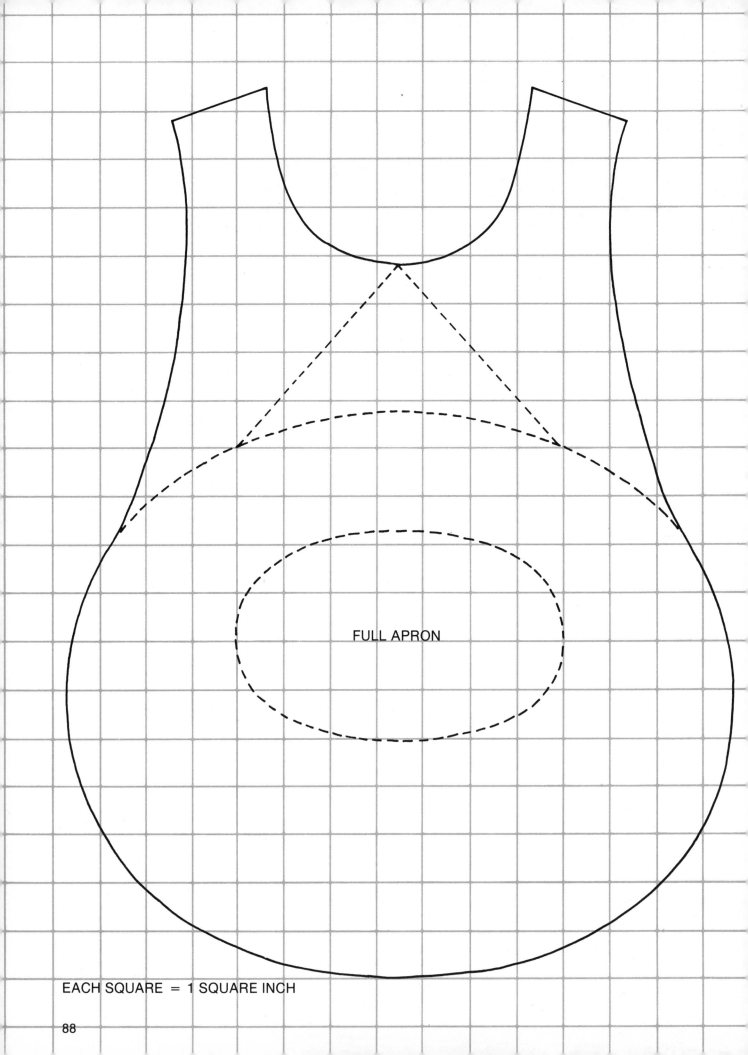

FULL APRON

EACH SQUARE = 1 SQUARE INCH

88

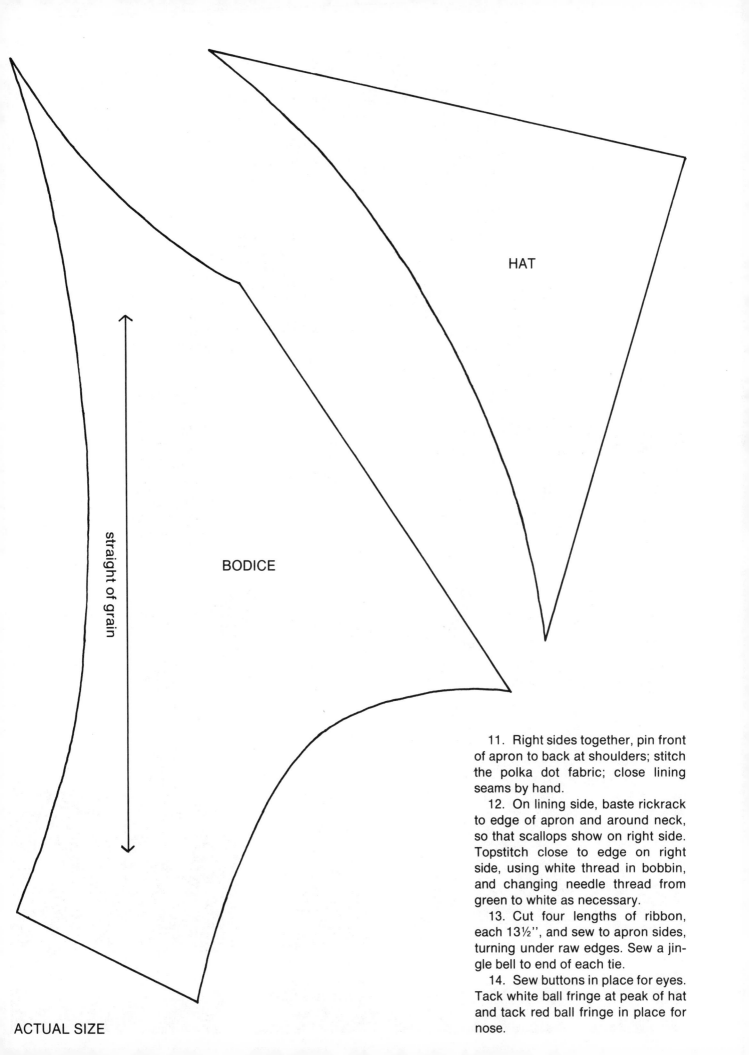

HAT

BODICE

straight of grain

11. Right sides together, pin front of apron to back at shoulders; stitch the polka dot fabric; close lining seams by hand.

12. On lining side, baste rickrack to edge of apron and around neck, so that scallops show on right side. Topstitch close to edge on right side, using white thread in bobbin, and changing needle thread from green to white as necessary.

13. Cut four lengths of ribbon, each 13½'', and sew to apron sides, turning under raw edges. Sew a jingle bell to end of each tie.

14. Sew buttons in place for eyes. Tack white ball fringe at peak of hat and tack red ball fringe in place for nose.

ACTUAL SIZE

Four fat little calico cookies march across the bottom of this Christmas apron. The ginger people are first embroidered and then appliqued with blanket stitches—but you could use zigzag machine stitches if you would rather. If you want the cook-

ies to look puffy, tuck in a little polyester stuffing before you complete the applique. Edging and apron ties are bias strips of the same brown calico. The apron is completely lined to give it extra body and make it opaque.

COOKIE APRON

MATERIALS

½ yard white pique (36'' or 45'' wide)
½ yard brown calico (45'' wide)
2 yards shirred white eyelet lace (⅝''wide)
Black, brown, pink embroidery thread
Polyester stuffing (optional)
1 yard narrow green ribbon

DIRECTIONS

1. On tracing paper, enlarge patterns for apron and pocket. Trace actual-size pattern for ginger cookie. Cut out patterns. (Note: To fit a taller child, you can add up to 4'' extra length at bottom.)

2. Fold white pique and cut out apron front and lining. Cut out pocket on fold. (No seam allowance is needed—outlines are cutting lines.)

3. From brown calico, cut true bias strips 2'' wide; seam them together to make three strips about 50'' long, leaving one strip about 24 inches long (see sketches in How-to Section). Press seams flat. Fold strips lengthwise right side out and press; then fold each edge to center, making bias edging ½'' wide.

4. Trace ginger cookie pattern four times on remaining scraps of calico; do not cut out yet. Transfer embroidery details (see directions in How-to Section). Use two strands embroidery thread for all embroidery. Satin-stitch black eyes and buttons; satin-stitch pink cheeks and embroider mouth with pink outline stitch.

5. With sewing machine, stitch around outline of each cookie; cut out, adding ¼'' hem allowance. Clip curves, clip into V-angles, turn under hem allowance and baste. (If

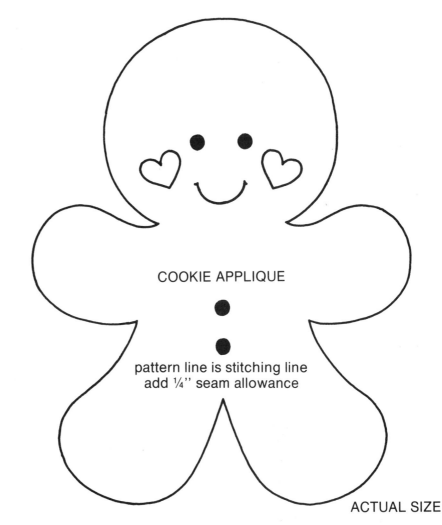

COOKIE APPLIQUE

pattern line is stitching line
add ¼'' seam allowance

ACTUAL SIZE

you baste with matching thread you won't have to rip out basting after you do applique.)

6. Pin cookies to apron front, placing them about 1½'' from bottom edge. Applique with small blanket stitches using two strands brown thread. For a puffy look, push a little polyester stuffing under the calico before you stitch it down.

7. Pin apron front to lining right sides out, and baste around edges. Bind edges by hand or machine with calico bias strips. Use one long strip to go around sides and bottom, mitering corners. Bind top with short

piece. Finally, bind the curve sides of the apron with the remaining two long pieces of bias, letting ends extend beyond curves to form neck and waist ties of equal length. Adjust length of ties to fit child and finish with invisible hand stitches.

8. Bind raw edges of folded pocket with remaining calico bias. Sew pocket to bib of apron.

9. Sew ruffle around edge of apron by hand.

10. Cut green ribbon in four equal lengths, tie into small bows and tack under chins of ginger cookies.

91

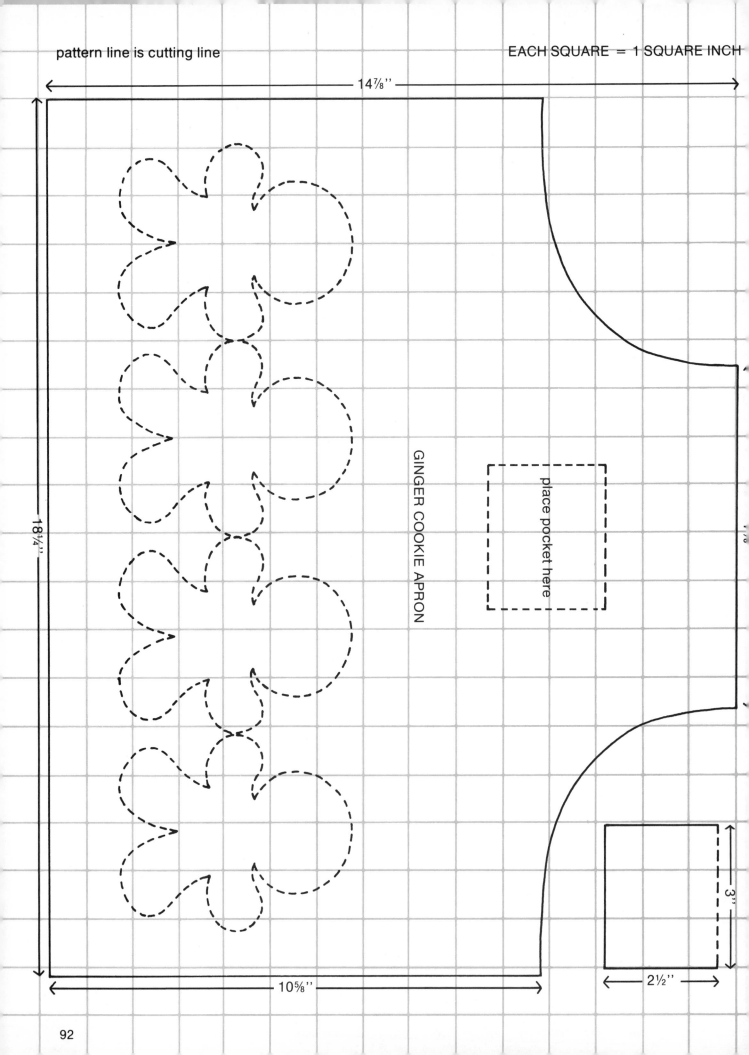

pattern line is cutting line

EACH SQUARE = 1 SQUARE INCH

14⅞''

18¼''

GINGER COOKIE APRON

place pocket here

10⅝''

3''

2½''

92

pattern line is stitching line
add ¼'' seam allowance

EACH SQUARE = 1 SQUARE INCH

16¾''

place on fold

CHIMNEY STRAP

15½''

⅞''

8⅛''

⅝''

ribbon

3⅝''

ROOF

14½''

⅝'' ribbon

HOUSE

1''

1⅜''

1''

1⅜''

ribbon

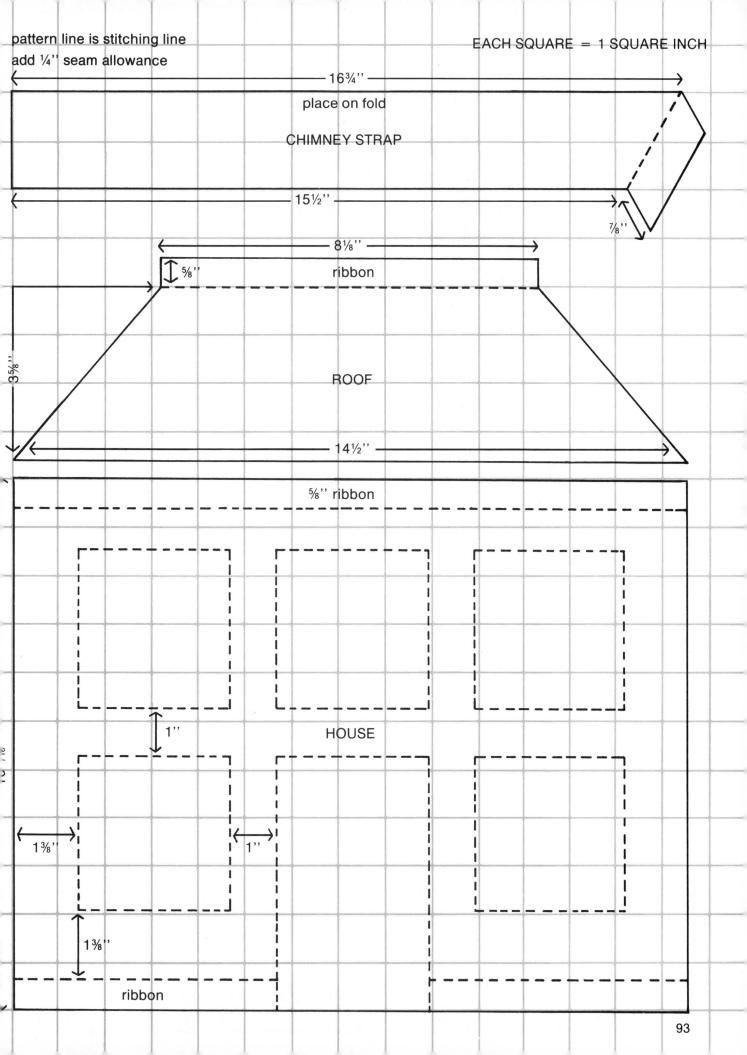

A house apron with door and window pockets could hold many tiny gift surprises! Fabric amounts and directions are given for making double-layer pockets; this will avoid show-through if fabrics are lightweight, and pockets will be sturdy.

The very tall chimneys on each side of the house become shoulder straps. They crisscross at the back, with casings at the ends to hold the ribbon ties.

For a neat finish, the apron is completely lined.

HOUSE APRON

MATERIALS

Yellow scrap, 18x7''
Red and pink checked scrap, 11x18''
Pink scrap 16x28'' (or ½ yard fabric, 36'' or 45'' wide)
Red polka dot scrap, 16x5''
Red scrap, 12x4½''
Red jumbo rickrack, 24''
1 package wide white bias tape
2⅜ yard white grosgrain ribbon (⅝'' wide)

DIRECTIONS

1. On tracing paper, enlarge pattern pieces following directions in the How-to Section; cut out. Make pattern for apron lining by butting roof edge to top of house.

2. Fold yellow fabric and cut five double pockets. Mark pockets for location of window panes. Cut ten pieces of wide bias tape 3'' long; fold tape lengthwise and baste to windows to make panes; machine stitch tape on both edges. Bind windows with remaining bias tape, mitering corners; stitch around inner edges of tape. Set aside.

3. From pink fabric, cut house front and entire back (lining) of apron, adding ¼'' seam allowance. Mark house for location of windows and door.

4. Cut roof from red polka dot fabric, adding ¼'' seam allowance. Fold red fabric and cut door (fold is at top of door pocket); add ¼'' seam allowance on cut edges. Right sides together, stitch side seams; leave bottom open; turn and press. Set aside.

5. Fold red check fabric and cut two chimney straps adding ¼'' seam allowance. Right sides together, stitch each strap, leaving straight end open for turning. Clip corners; clip into V-areas. Turn straps right side out; press. Fold under shaped end to make casing for ribbon ties; stitch. Set aside.

6. Right sides together, pin roof to house front; stitch; press seam open.

7. Right sides together, pin house front to apron lining. Stitch around outside edge, leaving roof top of apron open. Clip corners, turn and press.

8. Stitch 15'' length of white ribbon along bottom edge of house, tucking in raw ends. Pin door and window pockets in place; topstitch, leaving tops of pockets open.

9. At top of apron, turn under seam allowances on roof and lining. Insert straps in roof opening (see sketch for placement); pin and baste to close roof seam. Cut lengths of rickrack and ribbon 8½'' long; lay rickrack along top edge of roof; overlap with ribbon; baste, tucking in raw ends. Topstitch both edges of ribbon, closing seam and securing straps and rickrack.

10. Pin remaining length of white ribbon over seam between roof and house, with an extra 20'' on each side to make apron ties. Tuck rickrack under ribbon; topstitch both edges of ribbon.

11. Cross straps at back and thread ribbons through casings.

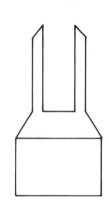

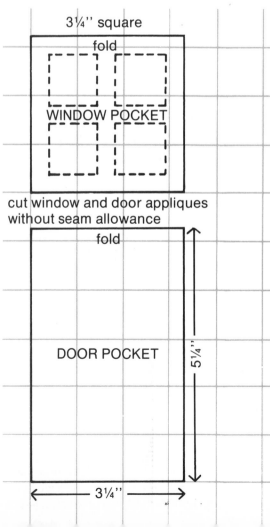

3¼'' square

fold

WINDOW POCKET

cut window and door appliques without seam allowance

fold

DOOR POCKET

5¼''

3¼''

CHRISTMAS STOCKINGS

When you need to rest and relax during the Christmas rush, sit down with a lapful of bright felts and yarns and make Christmas stockings for your family. A few hours embroidering while you visit with friends or listen to Christmas carols will soothe your nerves. Besides, think of the fun presenting personality stockings to the people you cherish. My Texas-born husband keeps his cowboy boot hanging over his desk; we move it to the fireplace on Christmas Eve.

If you collect the materials and then find you've run out of time, you can skip the handwork and use your sewing machine. In a pinch, you could even stick on the appliques with white glue—and resolve to add the blanket stitches next year!

Pattern outlines are cutting lines for felt, but stitching lines for other fabrics—add seam and hem allowances if you cut stockings from any woven fabric.

The seams around edges of felt stockings are blanket-stitched (not machine stitched); spacing stitches close together—¼'' deep, ⅛'' between each stitch—will make a strong and decorative edging.

high button shoe

MATERIALS

Green felt, 18x24''
Black felt, 15x3''
Felt scraps: light green, 6x7''; lavender, 3x9''; yellow-orange, 3x3½''; bright pink, 3x5''; aqua, 5x5''
3-ply crewel yarn: 8 yards black; 3 yards light green; 2 yards lavender; 1 yard yellow-orange; 1 yard bright pink; 2 yards aqua; 1 yard white
White eyelet ruffle, ¾'' wide, 12''
10 white ball buttons (½'' or ⅝'') or 10 jingle bells

DIRECTIONS

1. On tracing paper, enlarge pattern for shoe following directions in How-to Section. Trace actual-size patterns for flower appliques. From enlarged shoe pattern, trace pattern for shoe sole and heel lift. Cut out patterns.

2. From green felt, cut two shoe pieces. From black felt, cut shoe sole and heel lift. Cut flower and leaf appliques from colored felt scraps. To transfer embroidery design to shoe front, see directions in How-to Section.

3. Pin applique flowers to shoe front, following pattern for placement; when you've got it right, secure each piece with a few dots of white glue. Applique edges with blanket stitches, matching yarn colors to felt colors.

4. With white yarn, embroider vamp lines with backstitch. With light green yarn, chain-stitch flower stems.

5. Glue sole and heel lift to shoe and applique with black blanket stitches along top edges (bottom edges will be blanket-stitched in step 6).

6. Pin shoe front to back and sew them together by blanket-stitching all outside edges with black yarn. At top of shoe, blanket-stitch front and back edges separately, to leave shoe open.

7. Sew white buttons to right front edge of shoe, spacing them 1½'' apart. Sew eyelet ruffle to curved top edge of shoe, tapering it at the sides.

8. Braid nine lengths of black yarn to make a small loop for hanging shoe; attach at top left corner.

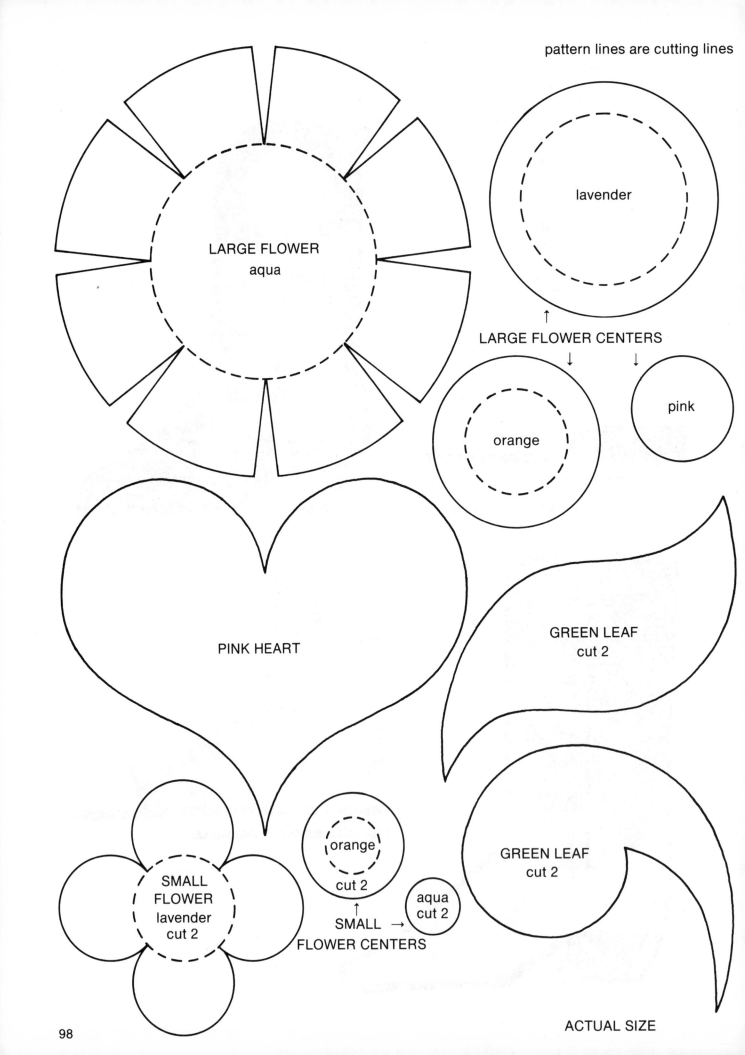

pattern lines are cutting lines

LARGE FLOWER
aqua

lavender

↑
LARGE FLOWER CENTERS
↓   ↓

orange

pink

PINK HEART

GREEN LEAF
cut 2

GREEN LEAF
cut 2

SMALL
FLOWER
lavender
cut 2

orange
cut 2

↑
SMALL →
FLOWER CENTERS

aqua
cut 2

ACTUAL SIZE

EACH SQUARE = 1 SQUARE INCH
pattern lines are cutting lines

BOOT FRONT AND BACK
(back is not decorated)

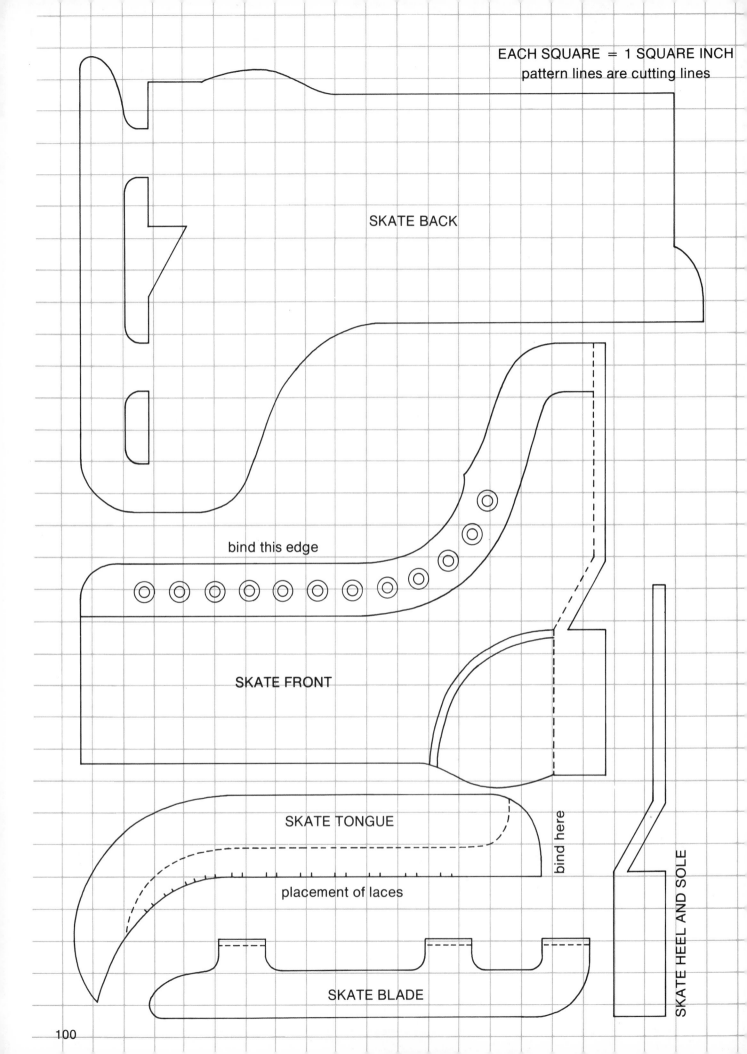

EACH SQUARE = 1 SQUARE INCH
pattern lines are cutting lines

SKATE BACK

bind this edge

SKATE FRONT

SKATE TONGUE

bind here

placement of laces

SKATE HEEL AND SOLE

SKATE BLADE

ice skate

MATERIALS

White felt, 18x30''
Gray felt, 15x3''
Black felt, 14x2½''
3-ply crewel yarn: 12 yards orange; 6 yards dark gray; 7 yards light gray; 3 yards pink
2 yards pink velvet ribbon (¼''or ¾'' wide)
2 jingle bells

DIRECTIONS

1. On tracing paper, enlarge pattern for skate following directions in How-to Section; cut out patterns.

2. From white felt, cut skate front, back and tongue. Cut skate runner from gray felt and heel and sole from black felt. To transfer embroidery details to skate front, see directions in How-to Section.

3. With pink yarn, embroider heel lines and line behind eyelets with backstitch.

4. Make bindings for skate and tongue. Cut strips of white felt ¾'' wide: 22'' long for skate, 4'' long for tongue. Press each binding in half lengthwise. Baste the long strip to top and front edge of skate, ending near bottom eyelet. Baste short strip to top curve of tongue. Sew bindings with backstitch embroidery using pink yarn.

5. With dotted line as a guide, pin tongue under front skate edge and check its position by laying skate front piece over back piece—they should line up exactly. Secure tongue to skate with a few dots of white glue; then sew tongue to skate front with invisible hand stitches under edge of binding.

6. Cut out centers of eyelets (⅜'' holes) and finish with buttonhole stitch, using light gray yarn.

7. Cut pink ribbon: one piece 3''; two pieces 3½''; eight pieces 4¼'' and one piece 24''. Starting with shortest piece on lowest eyelet, thread ribbons through eyelets; fold

around front edge of skate; tack both ends on back. Pull long length of ribbon through top eyelet and tie in bow at front. Sew a jingle bell to each end of ribbon.

8. Glue sole to skate front and applique with black blanket stitches along top edge of sole (bottom edge will be blanket-stitched in step 9).

9. Glue gray runner to skate back. Lay skate front over back and pin. Sew them together by blanket-stitching all edges, using dark gray yarn on gray runner, black on bottom (sole) of skate, and light gray on white shoe.

10. Braid nine lengths of light gray yarn to make a loop for hanging skate; attach at top left corner.

11. With orange yarn, make a 3'' pom-pom. Use the large-size pom-pom maker if you have one; or wind yarn around a strip of cardboard 1½'' wide, slide a needle under yarn along one edge and draw it together; cut yarn free on opposite edge; tie tightly. Attach to skate.

cowboy boot

MATERIALS

Dark gray felt, 18x30''
Tan felt, 18x12''
3-ply crewel yarn: 10 yards tan; 10 yards black; 2½ yards white

DIRECTIONS

1. Enlarge patterns on tracing paper following directions in How-to Section; cut out.

2. From gray felt, cut two complete boot pieces. Cut one tan vamp and one tan boot strap. To transfer embroidery design to boot front, see directions in How-to Section.

3. Chain-stitch scroll pattern on boot front with tan yarn. Chain-stitch vertical line with black yarn. (See embroidery stitches in How-to Section.)

4. Dab a little white glue on back of vamp, press to boot front (dotted lines show placement, ½'' from bottom edge of boot).

5. Embroider top and bottom edges (but not sides) of vamp to boot with backstitch, using white yarn. Stitches should be about ⅛'' long and ⅛'' from edge.

6. Pin boot front to boot back and sew them together by blanket-stitching outside edges with black yarn. At top of boot, blanket-stitch front and back edges separately, to leave boot open.

7. Embroider boot strap around edges with backstitch, using white yarn. Stitches should be about ⅛'' long and ⅛'' from edge. Fold over top of boot front and tack in place.

8. Braid nine lengths of black yarn to make a small loop for hanging boot; attach at top left corner.

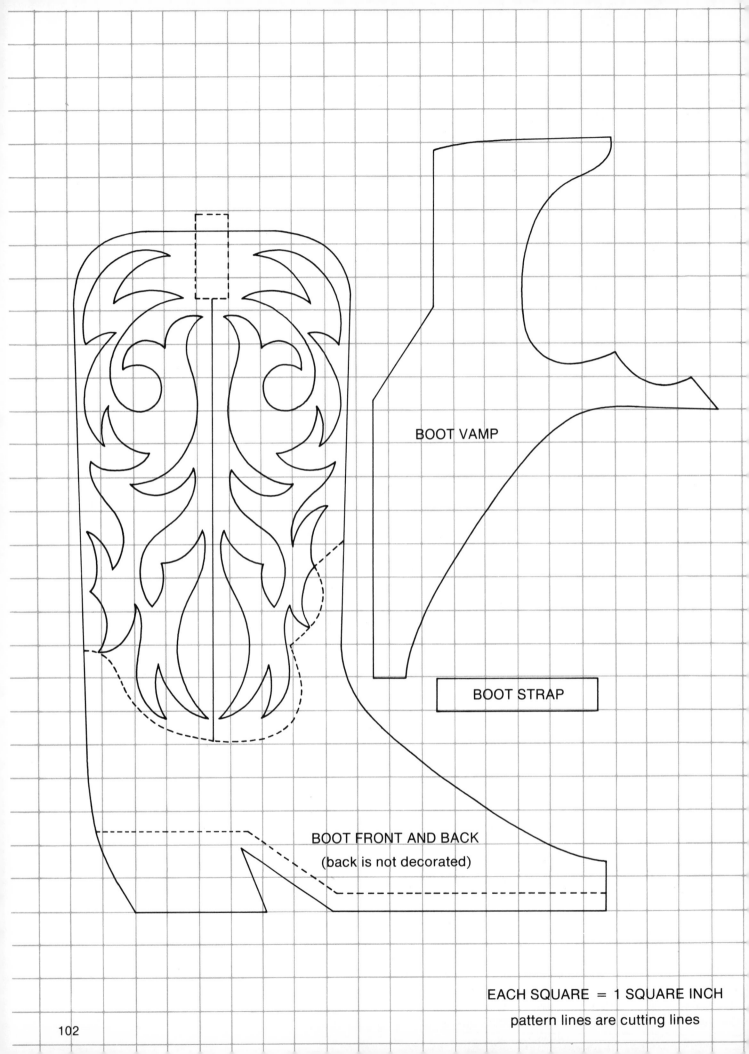

BOOT VAMP

BOOT STRAP

BOOT FRONT AND BACK
(back is not decorated)

EACH SQUARE = 1 SQUARE INCH

pattern lines are cutting lines

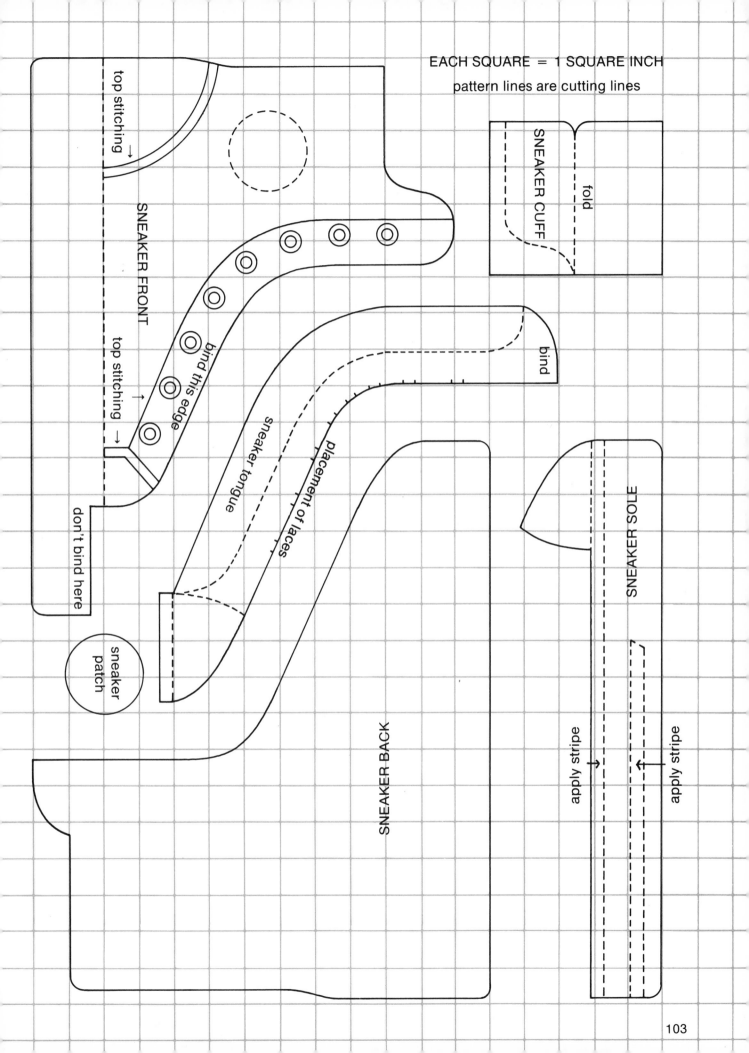

EACH SQUARE = 1 SQUARE INCH

pattern lines are cutting lines

SNEAKER CUFF

fold

top stitching ↓

SNEAKER FRONT

top stitching →

top stitching ↓

bind this edge

sneaker tongue

placement of laces

bind

don't bind here

sneaker patch

SNEAKER BACK

SNEAKER SOLE

apply stripe →

← apply stripe

sneaker

MATERIALS

White felt, 7x16''
Black felt, 28x2''
Blue felt, 13½x27''
3-ply crewel yarn: 9 yards white; 2 yards gray; 3 yards black; 4 yards blue
Pair white athletic shoe laces (at least 36'')

DIRECTIONS

1. On tracing paper, enlarge pattern for sneaker following directions in How-to Section; cut out patterns.

2. From blue felt, cut sneaker front, back and tongue. From white felt, cut sneaker sole, patch and cuff. To transfer applique and embroidery details to sneaker front, see directions in How-to Section.

3. With white yarn, embroider heel lines and line behind eyelets with backstitch. Glue circle patch in place and edge with white blanket stitches.

4. Make bindings for sneaker and tongue. Cut strips of black felt ¾'' wide: 28'' long for sneaker; 3'' long for tongue. Press each binding in half lengthwise. Baste the long strip to top and front edge of sneaker, ending at sole line (do not bind sole). Baste short strip to top curve of tongue. Sew bindings with backstitch embroidery using white yarn.

5. With dotted line as a guide, pin tongue under front sneaker edge and check its position by laying sneaker over back piece—they should line up exactly. Secure tongue to sneaker with a few dots of white glue; then sew tongue to sneaker front with invisible hand stitches under edge of binding. (Toe area will be filled in later, when sole is added in step 7.)

6. Cut out centers of eyelets ($^5/_{16}$'' holes) and finish with buttonhole stitch using light gray yarn.

7. Fold white cuff in half; pin under top edge of sneaker using dotted line as guide; sew cuff to sneaker with hand stitches hidden underneath binding; stitch through both layers of cuff.

8. Using dotted line as a guide, glue white sole to sneaker front. From black felt, cut two stripes ⅜'' wide: 15½'' long and 10'' long. Glue the long stripe to upper edge of sole. Cut one end of shorter stripe on a slant, and glue it to sole (see dotted lines for placement). Embroider edge of stripes with black blanket stitches. With white yarn, blanket-stitch inside edge of toe.

9. From one shoelace, cut seven pieces 4¼'' long. Starting at lower eyelet, thread laces through eyelets; fold around front edge of sneaker; tack both ends on back. Cut a 13'' piece from second shoelace; pull it through top eyelet and tack on back. Cut 11½'' piece from the other end of shoelace and tack it to back of tongue. Tie laces in a bow.

10. Pin sneaker front to back; sew them together by blanket-stitching all edges; use blue yarn on blue felt; white on white sole and cuff. At top of shoe, blanket-stitch front and back edges separately; to leave shoe open.

11. Braid nine lengths of black yarn to make a loop for hanging sneaker; attach at top left corner.

TREE ORNAMENTS

Here are designs for fifteen favorite Christmas motifs—the symbols that signal "Christmas is coming" to children everywhere.

In your family, you may have more ideas for shapes to cut out and stitch from bright-colored felts or other fabric scraps. Borrow designs wherever you find them to create your own Christmas motifs—and memories. Some other ornament possibilities in this book include the Barn Bag animals, the angel from the Nativity scene or the trim on the ginger cookie apron.

Many hobby stores sell 9x12" pieces of felt in assorted colors. From those listed, you can make one each of all fifteen ornaments, decorated on one side. If you cut the felt economically, saving every scrap for ornament trims, you will also be able to cut a second set of fifteen ornaments (without backs) to applique to the Christmas banner shown on page 112.

TREE ORNAMENTS

MATERIALS

Felt pieces, 9x12" as follows:
3 white
2 red, 2 lime green
1 each: medium green, dark green, magenta, bright pink, very light pink, bright orange, medium orange, yellow-orange, yellow, light gray, lavender, royal blue, navy blue, brown
Embroidery thread to match or blend with all felt colors
Polyester stuffing
Small ball fringe (⅝" diameter)
6 white, 2 red

GENERAL DIRECTIONS

Patterns for ornaments are all actual size. If you cut ornaments from fabrics instead of felt, add ¼" seam allowance.

1. Trace patterns and cut them out carefully.

2. Trace pattern outlines directly on felt with ballpoint pen or white drawing pencil. Cut out felt pieces and mark front of ornaments for placement of applique trims and embroidery—see directions in How-to Section.

3. Use white glue (sparingly) to attach trims to front of ornament.

Applique each bit of trim to ornament with tiny (⅛") blanket stitches (or substitute running stitches). Use two strands matching (or blending) embroidery thread for all embroidery. See How-to Section for all stitches.

4. Complete as much embroidery as you can on the front of each ornament; then blanket-stitch front to back.

5. Braid three lengths embroidery thread (all six strands) to make loop ¾" long for hanging ornaments. Insert between front and back at top of ornament; sew to secure. Loop should match felt color.

6. Stuff ornament lightly before you complete stitchery around edges.

7. To prepare bows: edge felt with tiny blanket stitches and fold into a bow, matching dots—don't tie. Wrap a full strand of matching embroidery thread tightly around center of bow several times; knot in back and tack to ornament.

trumpet

1. Cut front and back from yellow felt. Braid loop from yellow thread. Cut out trims from colors noted on pattern.

2. Glue valves and keys, mouthpiece and bell trim to trumpet front. Applique all pieces with tiny blanket stitches.

3. Secure loop ¼" to left of valves. Pin front to back; blanket-stitch outside edges and stuff following general directions.

4. Prepare bow (step 7 in general directions) and tack to curved tube of trumpet.

bell

1. Cut front and back from yellow-orange felt. Braid loop from bright orange thread. Cut trims from colors noted on pattern.

2. Glue ring and wide bands to front. Glue narrow bands to wide bands. Applique all edges with tiny blanket stitches.

3. Secure loop; pin front to back; blanket-stitch outside edges and stuff following general directions.

4. Prepare bow (step 7 in general directions) and tack to ring at dot.

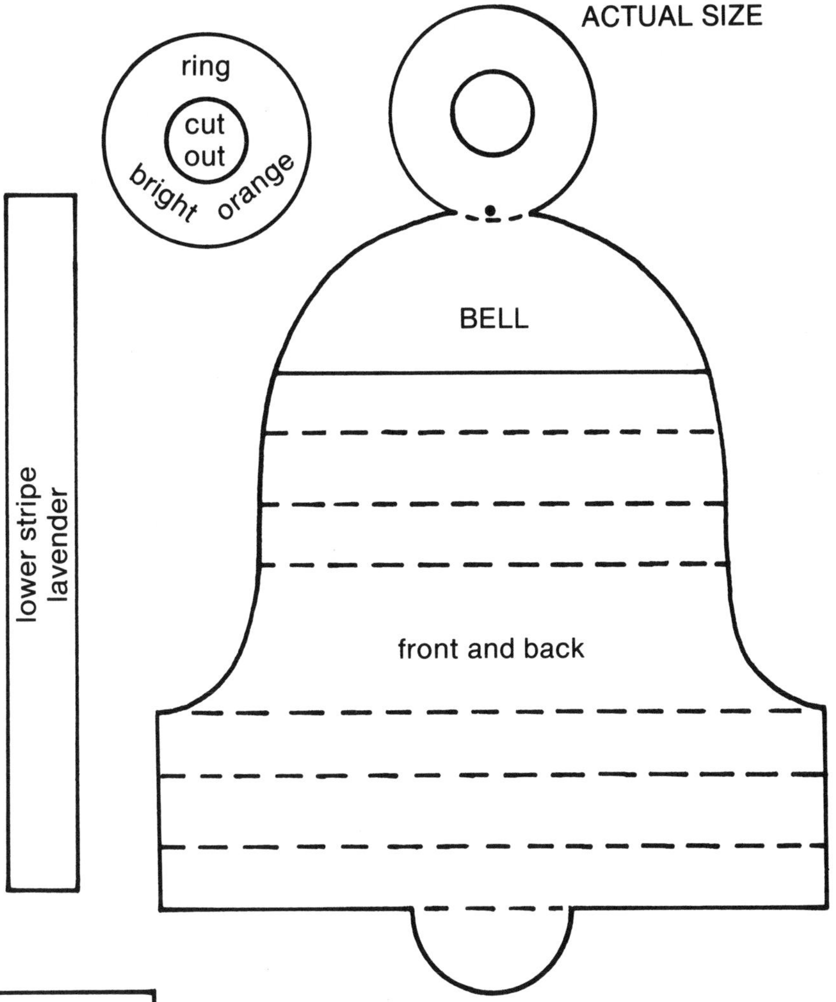

pattern lines are cutting lines

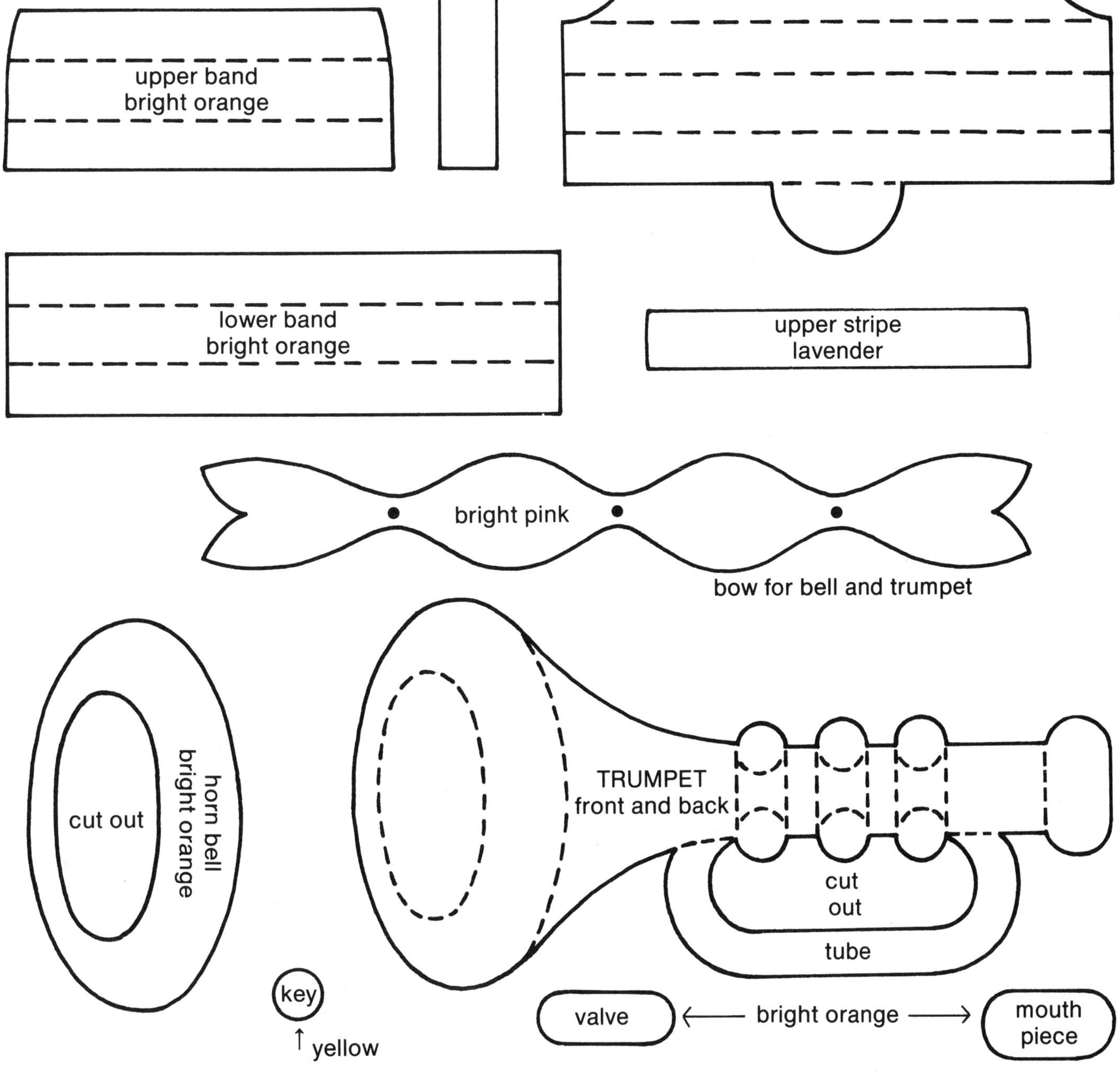

ring
cut out
bright orange

ACTUAL SIZE

BELL

lower stripe lavender

upper band
bright orange

front and back

lower band
bright orange

upper stripe
lavender

bright pink

bow for bell and trumpet

horn bell
bright orange

cut out

TRUMPET
front and back

cut out

tube

key

↑ yellow

valve ← bright orange → mouth piece

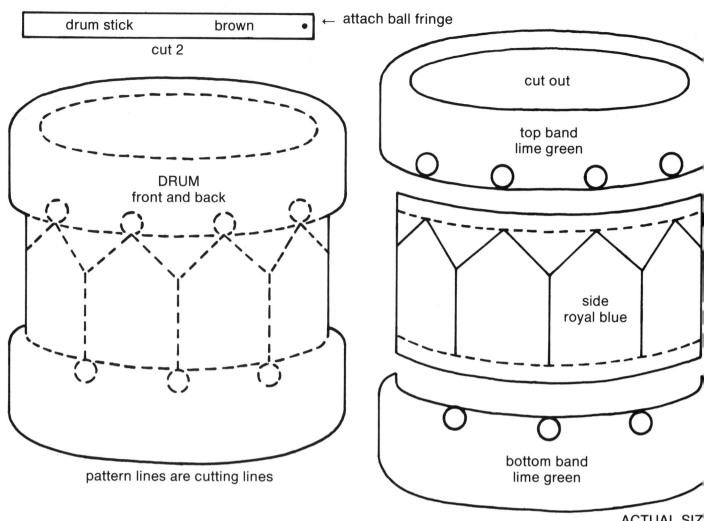

drum stick   brown   • ← attach ball fringe

cut 2

cut out

top band
lime green

DRUM
front and back

side
royal blue

bottom band
lime green

pattern lines are cutting lines

ACTUAL SIZ

drum

1. Cut drum front from white felt and drum back from royal blue. Cut drumsticks from a double-layer of brown felt (glue layers together before cutting); cut other trims as noted on patterns. Braid loop from lime green thread.

2. Glue royal blue side to front of drum, overlap with lime green top and bottom bands. Edge all appliques with tiny blanket stitches.

3. With white thread, chain-stitch line design on side of drum; with yellow-orange thread, satin-stitch drum lugs.

4. Edge drumsticks with blanket stitches and sew a white ball fringe to the end of each. Tack across top of drum.

5. Secure loop; pin front to back; blanket-stitch outside edges and stuff following general directions.

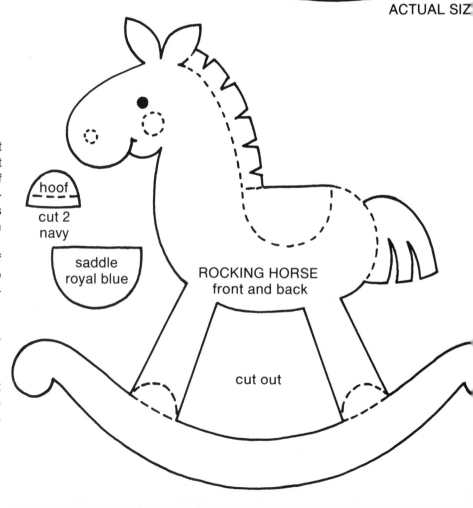

hoof
cut 2
navy

saddle
royal blue

ROCKING HORSE
front and back

cut out

cut out

skate

1. Cut front and back from white felt. Braid loop from white thread. Cut trims from colors noted on patterns.

2. Glue runner to skate front; glue sole in place overlapping runner. Applique edges with tiny blanket stitches.

3. Embroider heel and side of shoe with green running stitch. Blanket-stitch line along tongue with white. Make laces from six strands green thread; tie in bow at top and knot ends.

4. Attach loop. Pin front to back; blanket-stitch outside edges and stuff following general directions. Do not stuff runner.

5. Sew red ball fringe to toe.

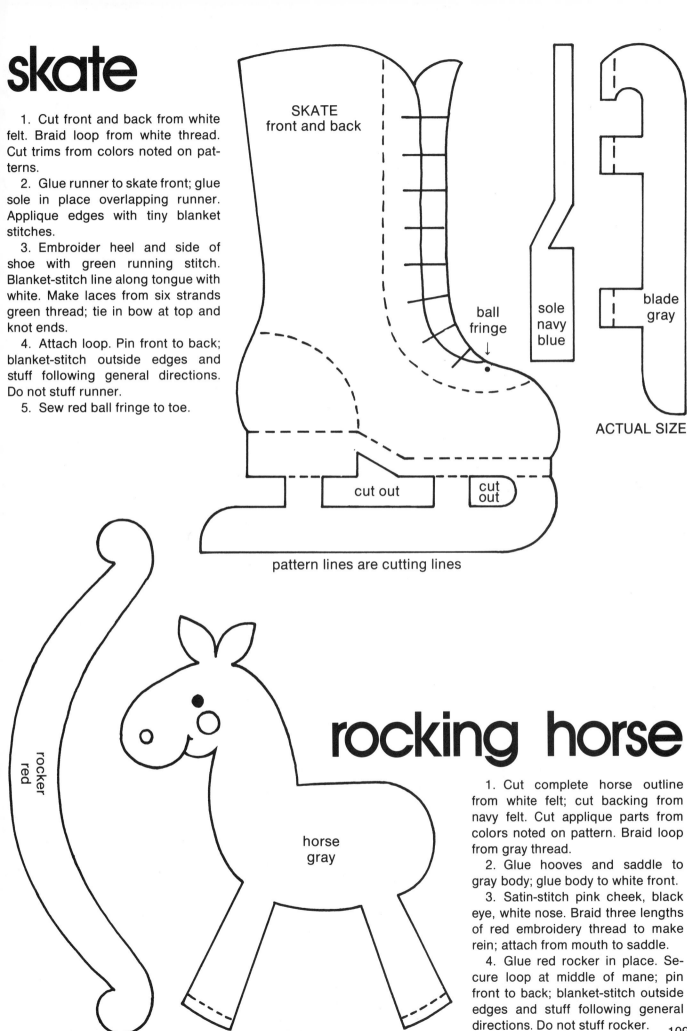

SKATE
front and back

ball
fringe

sole
navy
blue

blade
gray

ACTUAL SIZE

cut out

cut out

pattern lines are cutting lines

rocker
red

horse
gray

rocking horse

1. Cut complete horse outline from white felt; cut backing from navy felt. Cut applique parts from colors noted on pattern. Braid loop from gray thread.

2. Glue hooves and saddle to gray body; glue body to white front.

3. Satin-stitch pink cheek, black eye, white nose. Braid three lengths of red embroidery thread to make rein; attach from mouth to saddle.

4. Glue red rocker in place. Secure loop at middle of mane; pin front to back; blanket-stitch outside edges and stuff following general directions. Do not stuff rocker.

109

heel
magenta

paw
gray

cut 2

stocking
red

attach bow

CAT IN STOCKING
front and back

bow • medium green

toe
magenta

cuff
white

pattern lines are cutting lines

ACTUAL SIZE

cat in stocking

1. Cut front from gray felt; cut back from white felt. Cut applique parts from colors noted on patterns. Braid loop from gray thread.

2. Glue sock to front piece; glue heel, toe and cuff to sock. Glue paws in place on sock cuff. Applique all edges with tiny blanket stitches.

3. Embroider inner ears and nose with light pink and eyes with black satin stitch. Straight-stitch black eyebrows and white whiskers. Backstitch magenta mouth.

4. Secure loop; pin front to back; blanket-stitch outside edges and stuff following general directions.

5. Prepare bow (step 7 in general directions) and tack to cuff.

ear
yellow

cut 2

paw
yellow

TEDDY
front and back

mouse & candy cane

1. Cut front and back from lavender felt. Cut complete candy cane from magenta felt. Cut other applique pieces from colors noted on pattern. Embroider gift tag with black straight stitches before cutting out—it's easier. Braid loop from magenta thread.

2. On mouse face, satin-stitch black eye; backstitch red mouth. Embroider paw lines with black straight stitches.

3. Glue face and inner ears to front. Glue white stripes to magenta cane and glue cane to front, overlapping ear linings and face. Glue paws overlapping cane. Applique all pieces with tiny blanket stitches.

4. Secure loop at top of cane. Pin front to back; blanket-stitch outside edges and stuff following general directions.

5. Edge gift tag with white blanket stitches and tack to cane. Thread needle with six strands lime green embroidery thread and pass behind candy cane; tie long ends into a bow and knot ends.

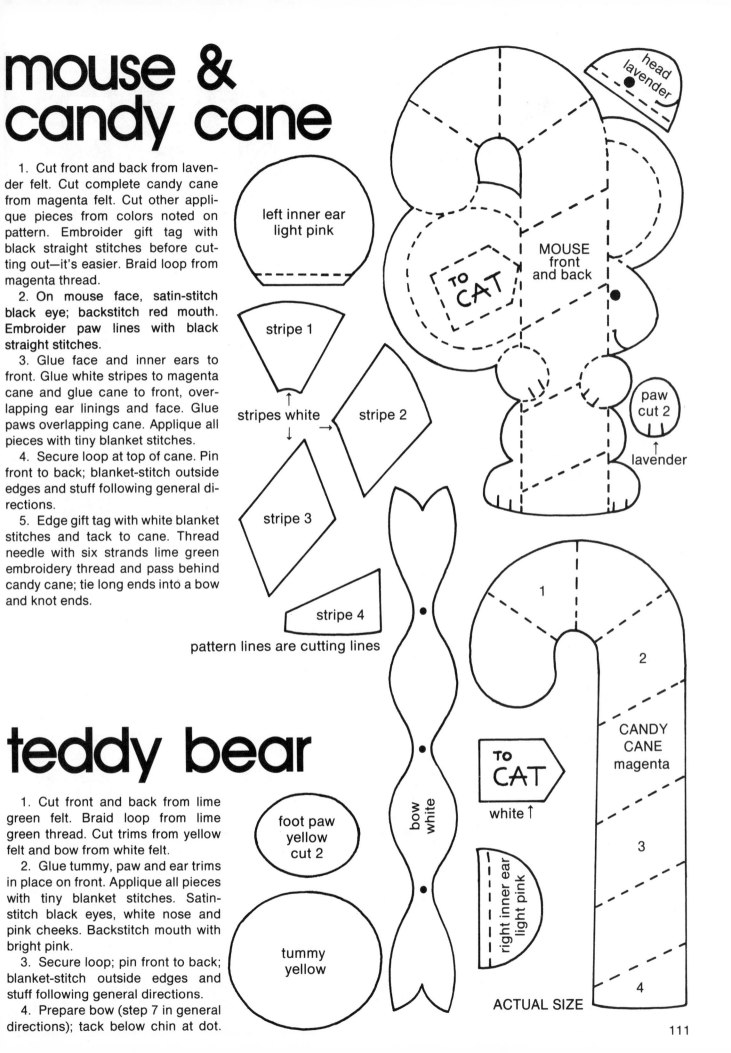

left inner ear
light pink

stripe 1

↑
stripes white
↓   →

stripe 2

stripe 3

stripe 4

pattern lines are cutting lines

head
lavender

MOUSE
front
and back

TO
CAT

paw
cut 2

↑
lavender

1

2

CANDY
CANE
magenta

3

4

TO
CAT

white ↑

bow
white

right inner ear
light pink

foot paw
yellow
cut 2

tummy
yellow

ACTUAL SIZE

teddy bear

1. Cut front and back from lime green felt. Braid loop from lime green thread. Cut trims from yellow felt and bow from white felt.

2. Glue tummy, paw and ear trims in place on front. Applique all pieces with tiny blanket stitches. Satin-stitch black eyes, white nose and pink cheeks. Backstitch mouth with bright pink.

3. Secure loop; pin front to back; blanket-stitch outside edges and stuff following general directions.

4. Prepare bow (step 7 in general directions); tack below chin at dot.

Are you looking for something extra-special to make, to auction off for big money at your next Christmas bazaar? This patchwork banner displays fifteen Christmas motifs appliqued to polka dot squares. It is padded with quilt batting and tied with jingle bells.

Work will go fast if members of your club each applique one square; then you could get together to piece the banner.

If you invest your time to make it for your own family Christmases, you'll want to store it carefully. Push some tissue paper under the loops of the bows to help them stay puffy. Roll the banner around the rod and protect it from dust with brown paper or a cleaner's plastic bag.

CHRISTMAS BANNER

MATERIALS

1¼ yard green fabric, 45'' wide
¼ yard white bird's-eye pique
⅝ yard aqua polka dot fabric
Thin polyester quilt batting 27x43''
  (optional, but desirable)
Felt in assorted colors (see listing
  under Ornaments)
24 brass-finish jingle bells
Brass-finish cafe curtain rod, ½''
  diameter, extending 28'' to 48''

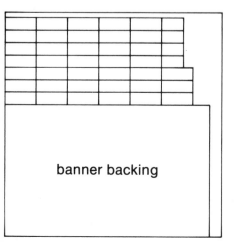

banner backing

DIRECTIONS

1. From green fabric, cut banner backing 42½x26½''. Cut 38 pieces, each 2½x6½''; cut four loops for hanging, 2½x4½''.

2. From white pique, cut 24 pieces, each 2½'' square.

3. From polka dot fabric, cut fifteen pieces, 6½'' square. Fabric sizes include ¼'' seam allowance.

4. To make felt appliques, follow patterns and directions for Tree Ornaments, omitting backs. Center each motif on a polka dot square; pin. Applique with tiny blanket stitches.

5. Piece the banner together by sewing horizontal strips first. Make six narrow strips, joining four white squares to three green rectangles, beginning and ending with white. Make four wide strips, joining four green rectangles to three polka dot squares, beginning and ending with green. Press seams toward darker fabric.

6. Pin horizontal rows together (refer to photo for placement); stitch; press seams toward darker fabric.

7. Make four hanging loops. Fold green fabric, right sides together; stitch across open end. Turn resulting tube right side out and press flat, placing seam at center back. To make loop, fold seam side inside. Pin and baste loops along top of banner over each white square—line up raw edge of loop even with raw edge of square.

8. Trim back piece if necessary to match size of pieced front; cut batting the same size.

9. On a flat surface layer batting, banner back (right side up) and front (wrong side up). Pin; baste around edges. Stitch ¼'' from edge, leaving about 10'' open on bottom edge for turning.

10. Turn right side out. Press edges flat. Close opening with invisible hand stitches.

11. Using six strands green embroidery thread, tack a brass jingle bell to the center of each white square; tie on banner back.

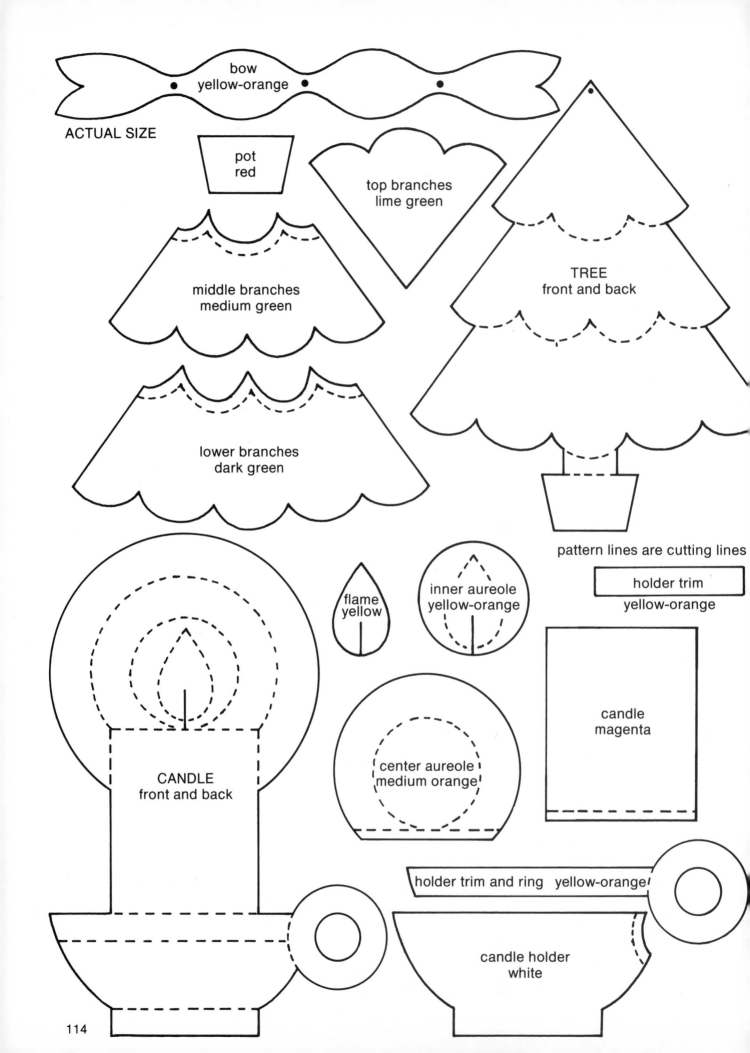

bow
yellow-orange

ACTUAL SIZE

pot
red

top branches
lime green

TREE
front and back

middle branches
medium green

lower branches
dark green

pattern lines are cutting lines

holder trim
yellow-orange

flame
yellow

inner aureole
yellow-orange

candle
magenta

CANDLE
front and back

center aureole
medium orange

holder trim and ring   yellow-orange

candle holder
white

tree

1. Cut tree front from brown felt and tree back from dark green felt. Cut branches and trim from colors noted on pattern. Braid loop from lime green thread.

2. Glue bottom, middle and top branches in place on tree front; also pot. Edge all appliques with tiny blanket stitches.

3. Secure loop. Pin front to back; blanket-stitch outside edges and stuff following general directions.

4. Prepare bow (step 7 in general directions) and tack to top of tree.

wreath

1. Cut front and back from dark green felt. Braid loop from dark green thread. Cut trims from colors noted on pattern.

2. Glue medium green and lime green pieces to front; applique edges with tiny blanket stitches.

3. Secure loop; pin front to back; blanket-stitch outside edges and stuff following general directions.

4. Prepare bow (step 7 in general directions) and tack to inner wreath opposite hanging loop.

candle

1. Cut front and back from bright orange felt. Braid loop from orange thread. Cut trims from colors noted on pattern.

2. Glue aureoles and flame to front. Glue candle, candle holder, and trim in place. Edge all appliques with tiny blanket stitches; chain-stitch black wick.

3. Secure loop. Pin front to back; blanket-stitch outside edges and stuff following general directions.

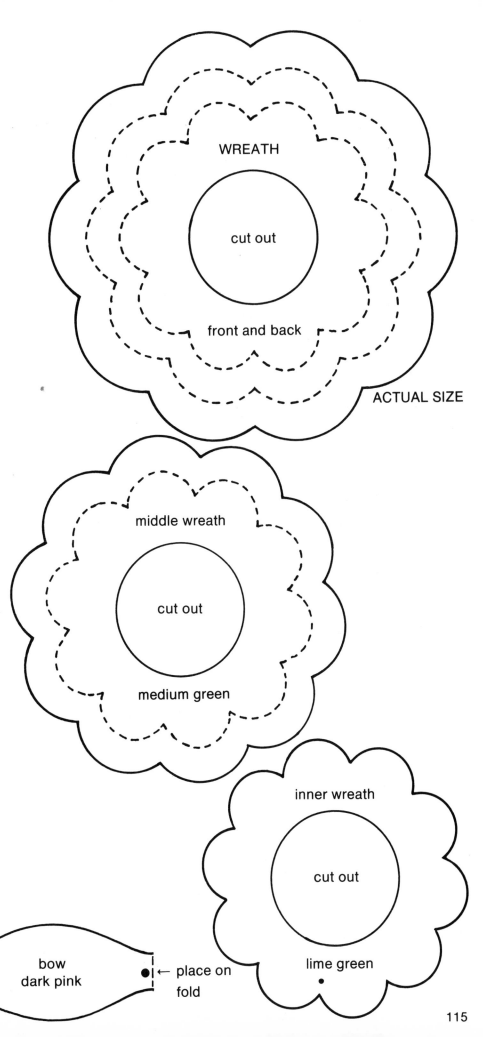

WREATH

cut out

front and back

ACTUAL SIZE

middle wreath

cut out

medium green

inner wreath

cut out

lime green

bow
dark pink

← place on fold

115

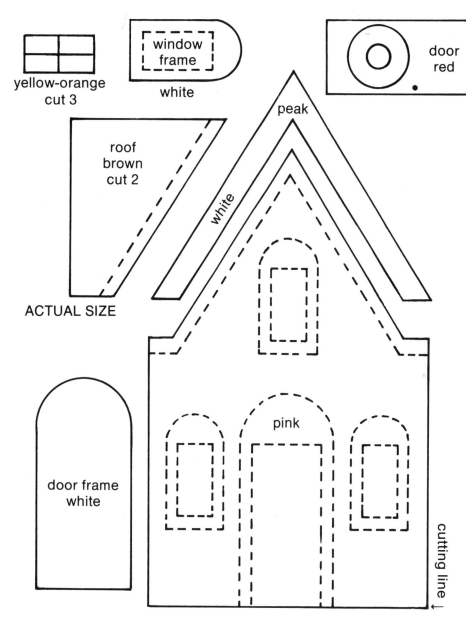

yellow-orange
cut 3

window
frame
white

door
red

roof
brown
cut 2

peak

white

ACTUAL SIZE

pink

door frame
white

cutting line ↓

house

1. Cut front from red felt; back from white felt. Cut house facade from bright pink, and other applique parts from colors noted on pattern. Braid loop from white thread.

2. Glue roof and house to front, butting edges. Glue white roof peak over butted edges. Glue window and door frames to house; glue windows and door to frames.

3. Edge all appliques with tiny blanket stitches. Chain-stitch white muntins across windows. Embroider lime green wreath on door with buttonhole stitches. Door knob is a brown French knot.

4. Secure loop to roof peak. Pin front to back; blanket-stitch outside edges and stuff following general directions.

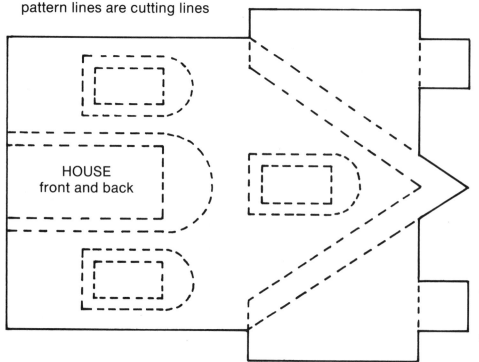

pattern lines are cutting lines

HOUSE
front and back

santa

1. Cut front from light pink felt; cut back from red felt. Cut applique parts from colors noted on pattern. Braid loop from white thread.

2. On pink front, embroider black eyes, bright pink cheeks, red nose, all satin stitch. Backstitch red mouth. Satin-stitch white buttons on suit.

3. Glue hat, suit and boots to front piece. Glue suit trim, cuffs and beard in place, overlapping suit. Applique all edges with tiny blanket stitches.

4. Secure loop; pin front to back; blanket-stitch outside edges and stuff following general directions.

5. Tack small white ball fringe to top of hat.

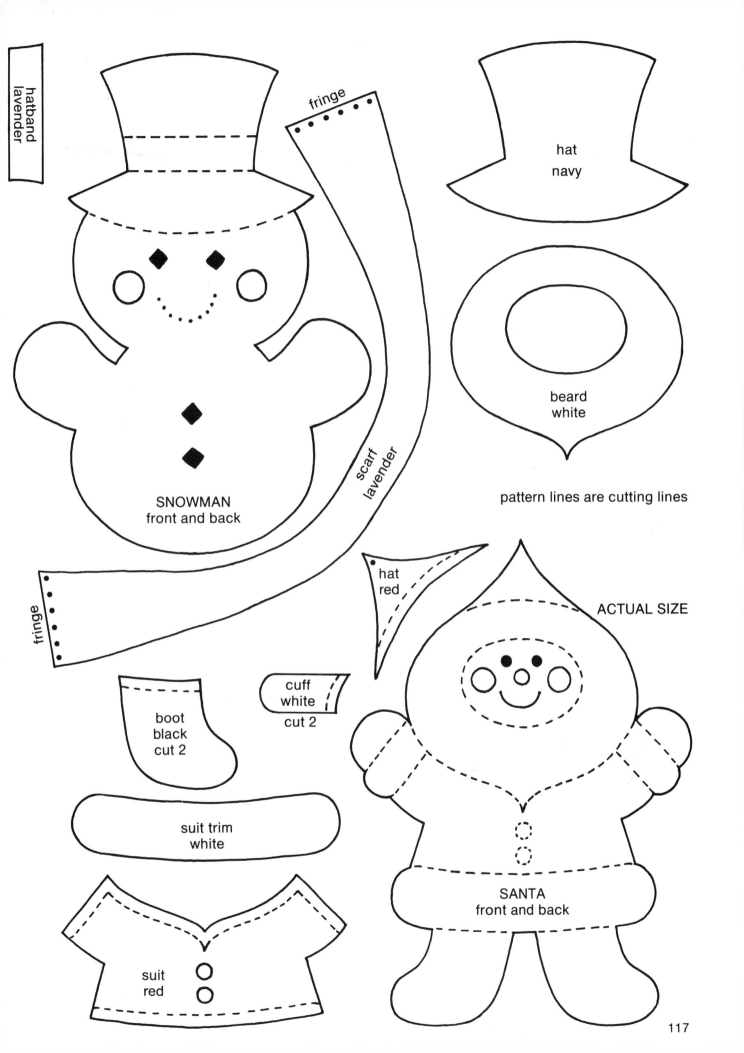

hatband
lavender

fringe

hat
navy

beard
white

pattern lines are cutting lines

scarf
lavender

SNOWMAN
front and back

fringe

hat
red

ACTUAL SIZE

cuff
white
cut 2

boot
black
cut 2

suit trim
white

SANTA
front and back

suit
red

117

ACTUAL SIZE

locomotive

engine
magenta

rear wheel
white
cut 2

window
white

front drive bar
royal blue

rear wheel
center
orange
cut 2

stack trim

orange ↑
↓

front
wheel
center
cut 2

front wheel
white
cut 2

window frame

cut out

magenta

1. Cut front from royal blue felt; cut back from navy felt. Braid loop from navy thread. Cut trims from colors noted on patterns.

2. Glue white window and magenta window frame to cab; glue magenta engine in place; trim engine and smokestacks with orange stripes. Glue white wheels in place; add orange centers and royal blue side rods. Edge all appliques with tiny blanket stitches.

3. Secure loop at top right corner of cab. Pin front to back; blanket-stitch outside edges and stuff following general directions. Stitch and stuff smokestacks first.

snowman

1. Cut front and back from white felt; cut trim from colors noted on pattern. Braid loop from navy thread.

2. Glue hat and hatband to front of snowman; applique with blanket stitches. Satin-stitch pink cheeks and black eyes and buttons; embroider smile with black French knots.

3. Secure loop; pin front to back; blanket-stitch outside edges and stuff following general directions.

4. Edge scarf with blanket stitches and attach navy blue fringes at dots on each end of scarf. Knot scarf around snowman's neck.

pattern lines are cutting lines

LOCOMOTIVE
front and back

engine trim
orange

stack trim
orange

royal blue
back drive bar

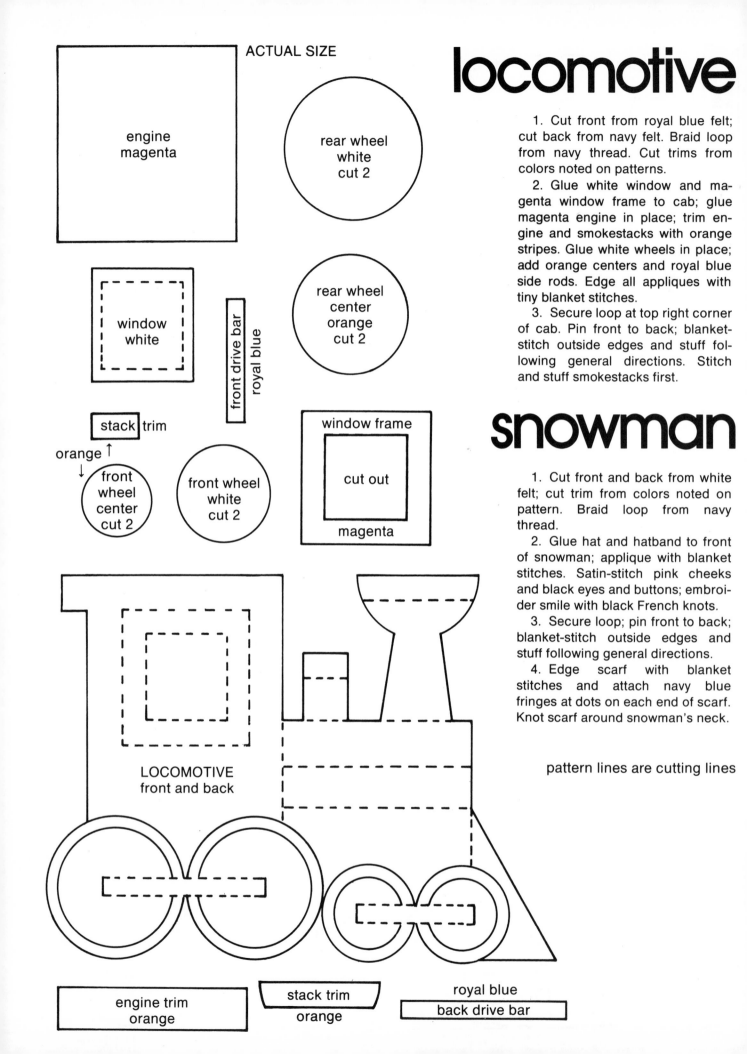

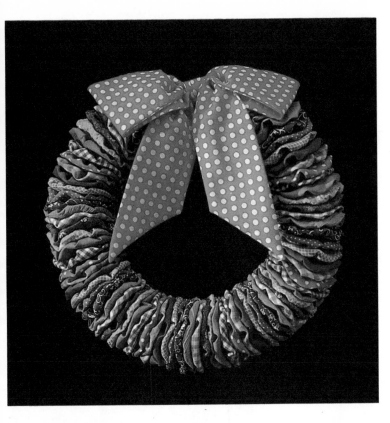

YO-YO WREATH

If you're a compulsive scrap saver, here's a way to use up every 6'' bit you've been hoarding "just in case." I had so many different green fabrics left over, I decided to buy a couple more quarter-yards—to make my wreath entirely of green prints and solids. But a multi-color wreath would be equally effective. Fabrics should not be too heavy. Broadcloth is ideal; poplin weight is a bit stiff for shirring.

Usually you hem edges of yo-yo circles, but you won't have to bother when you sew them for a wreath—they're pressed against each other and you don't see the raw edges.

This is a good "take-along" project because you can sew and shirr the circles by hand. Or stitch them on the machine and shirr them whenever you have a few minutes to sit and wait.

MATERIALS

¼ yard of eleven different fabrics (45'' wide), or ½ yard of four or five fabrics

¼ yard red print or polka dot fabric for bow
Wire coat hanger

DIRECTIONS

1. Use a compass to draw a 6'' circle on lightweight cardboard or sandpaper. Mark center. (Or trace around a 6'' plate on paper; cut out and fold in quarters to find center. Paste on cardboard.) Cut out pattern.

2. Trace pattern on one piece of fabric, crowding as many circles as you can—let sides touch. Mark centers. To cut four yo-yos at once, pin four layers of fabric together, pinning within perimeters of each circle. Cut out circles and pierce centers with a skewer or nail; make hole large enough to thread on coat hanger wire. Cut from eighty to ninety circles.

3. With largest machine stitch (or by hand) stitch on wrong side of fabric ¼'' from edge of circles. Overlap stitching at beginning and end. Turn

circle over. Pull bobbin threads to shirr tightly. Tie ends of threads and tuck inside opening.

4. With pliers or wire cutter, cut coat hanger below hook; you want a piece 32'' long. Wear old gloves to protect your hands. Bend a hook at each end; hook ends and form a circle 9½'' in diameter.

5. Straighten out one hook and thread finished yo-yos onto wire; yo-yos should all face the same direction. When wreath looks full, hook wires together, trimming them if necessary and pinching them flat with pliers.

6. To make bow, cut red fabric 6x36''; fold lengthwise, right sides together. Stitch ¼'' from edge, leaving a 3'' opening for turning. Ends of bow may be straight or angled.

7. Turn right side out; fold into bow shape and secure with thread. Tie to wreath over wire hooks. To finish bow, cut another piece 2x4''; turn under ¼'' on all sides; pleat center and wrap around bow, covering threads and wire hooks. Secure at back with hand stitches.

ACTUAL SIZE

pattern lines for sleigh are cutting lines

RUNNERS

cut out shaded areas

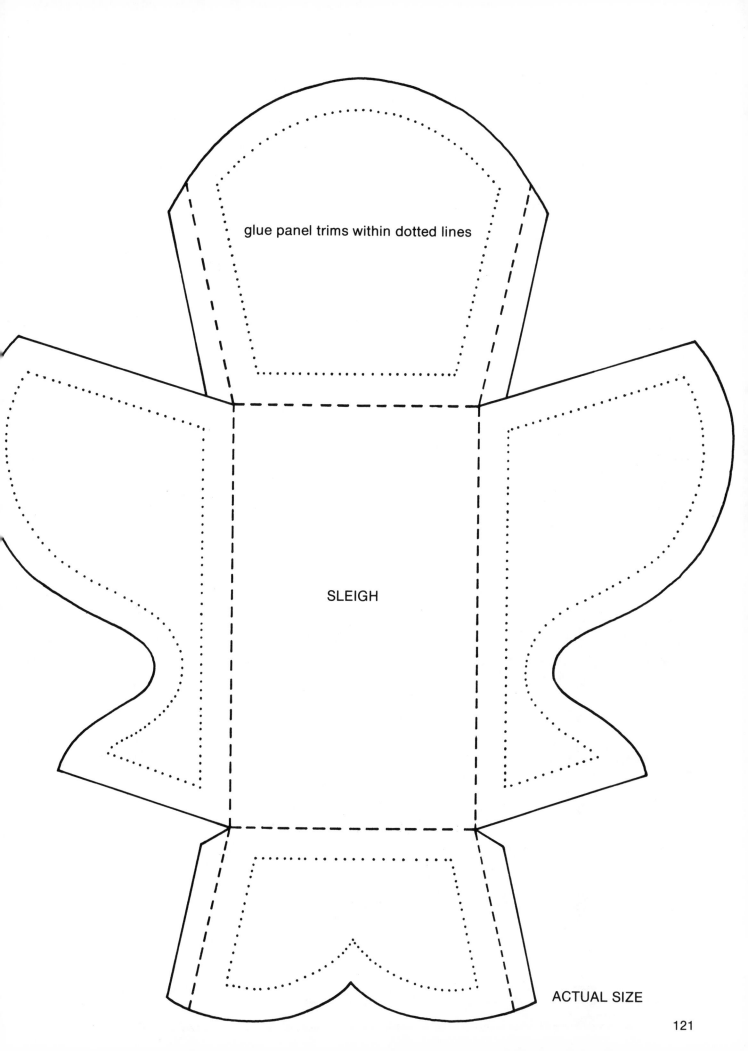

glue panel trims within dotted lines

SLEIGH

ACTUAL SIZE

Can you picture these eight tiny reindeer pulling their cardboard sleigh across your Christmas table or mantelpiece? Fill the sleigh with small presents (honest-to-goodness ones or empty boxes) or with Christmas greens and pine cones.

If you're short on time, make a pair of reindeer—one from tiny red checks, one from green checks. Or cut the team of eight from a scrap-bag variety of multi-colored prints; they would be charming!

The neatest way to cut the cardboard sleigh is with an X-acto knife, available at hobby and art stores. Get one fitted with a #11 blade. If you've never used this tool, practice on a scrap of cardboard first—and be careful to keep your holding hand a safe distance from the knife blade. Put a stack of newspapers under the piece you're cutting out, to protect the table top.

The sleigh can be trimmed with panels cut from plain brown paper if you don't have any striped fabric handy. In that case, you won't need the fusible web or white paper.

REINDEER & SLEIGH

MATERIALS FOR REINDEER

¼ yard brown and white polka dot fabric
¼ yard brown and white gingham check fabric
¼ yard white fabric
Brown felt, 7x10''
White felt, 7x10''
Black embroidery thread
Polyester stuffing
4 small white ball fringes
4 small brown ball fringes
1½ yards brown embroidered ribbon, ¾'' wide
1½ yards pink rickrack
1½ yards green rickrack

DIRECTIONS

1. Trace and cut out actual-size patterns. *Pattern lines are stitching lines.*

2. Pin underbody pattern to wrong side of white fabric; trace outline with pencil and transfer dart marks (see directions in How-to Section). Cut out underbody adding ¼'' seam allowance all around. Repeat for eight reindeer (or as many as you want to make).

3. Fold legs, right sides together, and stitch darts using very small machine stitches; secure beginning and end of stitching line. Trim dart parallel to stitching line. Set aside.

4. Fold dotted and checked fabrics, right sides together. Trace patterns for upper body four times on each fabric and cut out, adding ¼'' seam allowance all around. You'll have a total of sixteen upper bodies, four left and four right sides from each print. Mark dots for eye, under chin and at tail.

5. Right sides together, pin and baste each pair of upper body pieces from dot under chin to tail dot. Machine stitch and clip curves carefully.

6. Right sides together, pin underbody to upper body; baste and machine stitch, leaving 1'' open on one side of rump for turning. Clip curves; clip corners of feet.

7. Turn reindeer right side out and stuff firmly (a crochet hook will be helpful as a turning and stuffing tool). Close opening with invisible hand stitching.

8. Satin-stitch black eyes. Tack ball-fringe tails in place.

9. To make ears, trace ear pattern four times on both dotted and checked fabrics—both fabrics folded right sides together. Do not cut fabric before stitching. Stitch on outlines, leaving one side open for turning. Cut out ears and trim seam close to stitching line. Turn right side out and close opening with invisible hand stitches. Pinch and pleat fabric together in the middle and wrap thread around pleat tightly to form two ears. Tack ears to top of head.

10. Cut brown and white felts in half (5x7''). With rubber cement or fusible web, bond brown pieces together; bond white pieces together. Trace and cut out four white antlers and four brown antlers. (Outline is cutting line.) Fold each set of antlers at center; tack to head in front of ears, placing short horns forward . . . white antlers on polka dot bodies; brown antlers on checked bodies.

11. Cut rickrack and ribbon into 6'' lengths. Stitch pink rickrack to edges of four ribbons; stitch green rickrack to remaining four. Wrap pink-trimmed ribbon around middles of polka dot reindeer; tack. Wrap green-trimmed ribbon around middles of checked reindeer; tack.

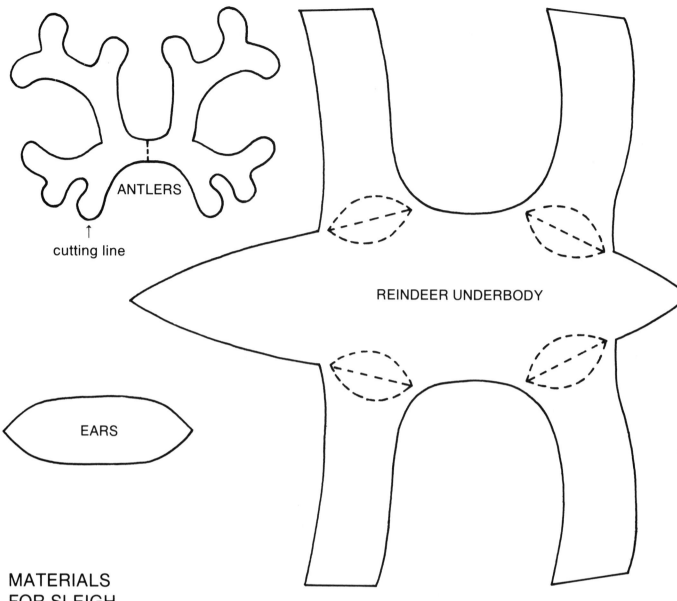

ANTLERS

↑
cutting line

EARS

REINDEER UNDERBODY

MATERIALS FOR SLEIGH

White lightweight cardboard,
  10x15''
White paper, 7x7''
Fusible web, 7x7'' or rubber cement
Brown and white striped fabric,
  7x7''
White glue
1¼ yards shiny green cord
Assorted pink and green fabric
  scraps and ribbons, for gift boxes

DIRECTIONS

1. Trace sleigh pattern onto cardboard and cut out with X-acto knife. Score folds by running knife lightly along fold lines, using a straightedge as a guide.

2. With fusible web or rubber cement, bond striped fabric to paper. On paper side, trace patterns for front, back and side panels of sleigh; flip pattern for side panel to get left and right sides. Cut out panels and glue to sleigh.

3. Fold sleigh on scored lines to shape it—striped design outside. Glue front and back flaps to inside of side panels.

4. Trace runner pattern onto cardboard; cut out design areas first; then cut out entire runner piece with X-acto knife. Score on fold lines; fold and glue flap to edge of runner. Glue assembled runner to bottom of sleigh.

5. Arrange reindeer in a double line. Starting with lead reindeer, hitch each line together by running cord through braid trim on outside; secure cord with a pin where it passes under trim on each reindeer. Tie ends of reins in knot.

6. Wrap tiny packages and pile in and around sleigh.

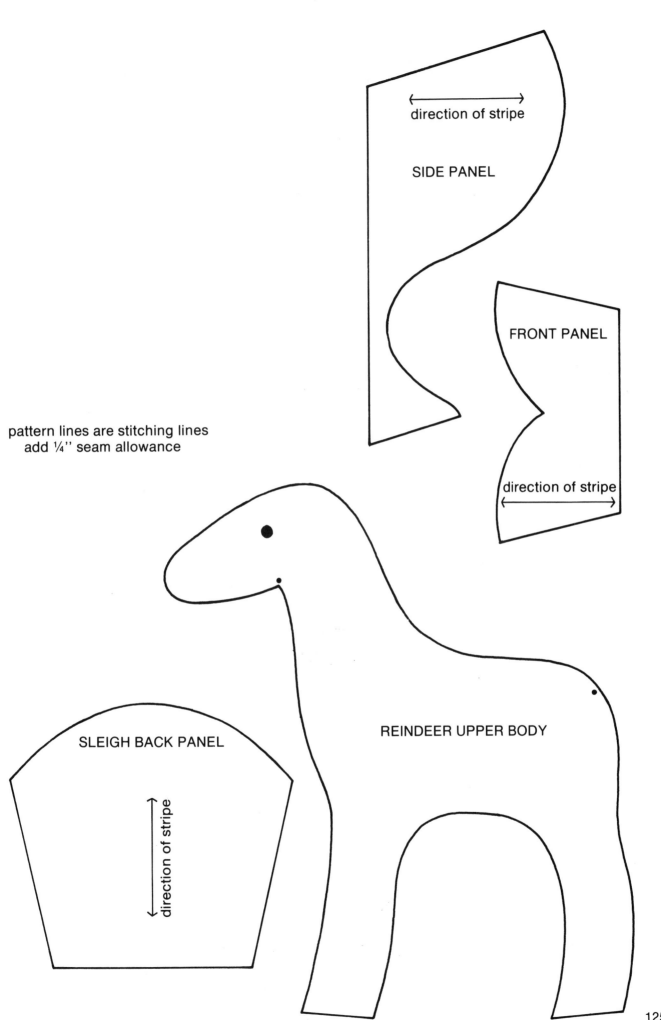

direction of stripe

SIDE PANEL

FRONT PANEL

direction of stripe

pattern lines are stitching lines
add ¼'' seam allowance

SLEIGH BACK PANEL

direction of stripe

REINDEER UPPER BODY

HOW-TO SECTION

If there's something about the patterns or sewing you don't understand or don't already know how to do (embroidery stitches or enlarging patterns), look it up here.

SUPPLIES AND TOOLS

You'll need shears and scissors for cutting paper, cardboard and fabric. You can also make good use of a small hobby knife with a sharp point, such as the X-acto knife with #11 blade. It's ideal for cutting out stencil details in cardboard, although you can make do with a single-edge razor blade.

Transparent tracing paper is a must for pattern-making (see below) and if you have it, dressmaker's carbon and a tracing wheel will be useful. You'll want a soft pencil and a ballpoint pen; maybe a soft white drawing pencil, too, for marking felt.

You'll need a ruler for tracing straight lines; if it's metal, you can also use it as a cutting edge with your X-acto knife. Also helpful: tape measure; yardstick; T-square or right angle for making perfect 90° corners, and a compass for drawing accurate circles.

Some designs call for bonding two materials together. You can use fusible web on almost all fabrics; follow package directions for applying heat. If you're layering felt, use a thin coat of white glue or rubber cement, or lightweight fusible web.

Along with threads and yarns to match your fabrics, you'll need pins and a selection of needles, some with large eyes for yarn embroidery.

Polyester quilt batting comes in two weights; you can substitute two thin layers for one thick. Save all the scraps for stuffing small toys.

For turning and stuffing tools, use what's handy. I find a crochet hook almost invaluable for turning legs and tails of small animals, and a long ruler or wooden spoon handle is equally handy for turning straps.

MAKING PATTERNS

Most of the patterns in this book are actual-size, ready for you to trace. A few are drawn on grids and need to be enlarged (directions follow). Some designs drawn half-size on a grid also include full-size patterns for the applique or embroidery details. For example, you can trace the face and ears (full-size) for the lion placemat. Then refer to the outline on the grid to enlarge and complete the pattern for mane and body.

The best paper for pattern-making is transparent tracing paper from art supply stores—you can find it in tablets or by the roll. The 36'' roll is wide enough to make any pattern in this book.

To enlarge patterns, rule your paper with 1'' squares. Copy the design outline from the small squares to the corresponding large squares, using the squares as a drawing guide.

If you are copying a large pattern, number the squares across the top and down one side. The numbers will make it easier to compare the large pattern with the small pattern.

Patterns with simple outlines are easy to enlarge, but if you have no confidence in your drawing ability, you can take the pattern to a photo copying service and get a photostat enlargement. To save money, ask for a "first print" which will be a negative on paper—otherwise you'll pay for two prints, a negative and a positive.

If there are several pieces to a pattern you've enlarged, check the pieces against each other for accuracy before you cut out fabric.

In trying to fit full-size patterns on 8½x11'' book pages, I've broken some patterns into pieces (goldfish; octopus). You'll find directions for butting the pieces together to make the complete pattern outline. Where both sides of a pattern are identical, I've drawn only half the pattern if that's all there's room for. When you trace it, trace it on folded paper, laying the "place on fold" edge on the fold. Cut it out; unfold the paper and you have the full-size pattern.

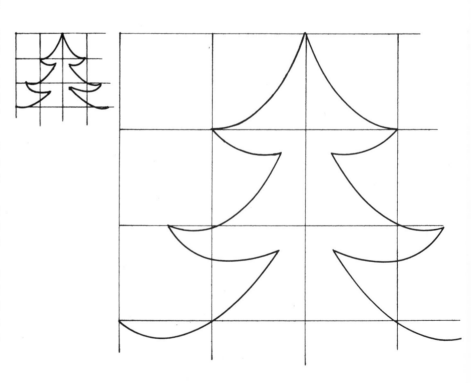

FABRICS

Use lightweight fabrics (broadcloth weight) for small figures like barn bag animals, and for appliques—especially smaller appliques. If fabric is too heavy or stiff, it's difficult to turn under seam allowances for appliques, or to turn small items right side out after stitching. Avoid fabrics that fray easily.

If the grain of fabric is important to the design, I've marked patterns to show straight-of-grain; I've also included cutting layouts for designs requiring a lot of pieces.

FELT

Felt has no grain, so you can lay out pattern pieces any which way, like a jigsaw puzzle, to conserve material. If the felt is creased, steam press before cutting—it shrinks. Do not wash felt articles; dry clean only.

Several patterns call for felt cutouts of double-thickness. Brush felt sparingly with white glue or rubber cement and press two layers together; then cut out pieces. You can also use lightweight fusible web, but it tends to make the felt rather stiff.

TRACING PATTERNS ON FABRIC

Lay patterns face down on the wrong side of fabric and trace around them with a pencil or ball-point pen. Leave ½'' space between each outline to allow for seams. Pattern outlines are stitching lines; when you cut fabric, add ¼'' seam allowance. (Felt is the exception; if your design or applique is cut from felt, pattern line is cutting line.)

If you will be using patterns more than two or three times, paste or trace them onto lightweight cardboard or fine sandpaper and cut them out.

TRANSFERRING EMBROIDERY DETAILS TO FABRIC

There are several ways to mark the face of fabrics for embroidery and placement of appliques. Choose the one best suited to your fabric—and your standards. I'm fussy about pen-cil lines showing on the face of fabric—so if I'm working on light colors, I'll trace the design lightly on the back, then baste along the tracing line to get the pattern outline on the face of the fabric.

If your pattern is on tracing paper, you can black the line on the back of the paper with soft pencil, lay the pattern on the face of the fabric and rub off the design with your fingernail or the rounded end of a pen. Or you can use dressmaker's carbon and a tracing wheel to transfer the outlines of large details. The rub-off technique and dressmaker's carbon do not always leave clear pattern outlines on felts. The best way to mark felt is to punch through the tracing paper with a ball-point pen, making dots on the felt along the pattern line. On dark felts, use a sharp-pointed white drawing pencil.

If your pattern is on heavy paper or lightweight cardboard, cut out the interior details (eyes, smiles, etc.) and use the pattern like a stencil to draw design lines on fabric.

APPLIQUES

Before you cut out applique pieces, decide whether you will attach them by hand or by zigzag stitching on your sewing machine. If you use the machine, cut fabric on pattern outlines—without seam or hem allowance. Use fusible web to attach the cutout to fabric; then secure the edges with closely-spaced zigzag stitches.

You can do more of your sewing in your lap (take-along projects) if you attach appliques by hand. Cut them out, adding ¼'' seam (hem) allowance; turn edges under and hold them under by finger-pressing, pressing with an iron or basting.

Technique will help you handle small pieces easily—especially the small circles. Before cutting them out, machine stitch or handstitch on the tracing line. This gives you a precise folding edge. Cut out pieces, adding ¼'' seam allowance; clip or trim seam allowance as you turn under hems. Better yet, cut circles with pinking shears—pinking trims out some of the bulk so edges turn under smoothly.

Pin applique cutouts to body fabric and baste in place. (If you didn't baste seam allowance when you turned it under, this basting will catch it.) Secure appliques with blind hemming (invisible stitches) or with embroidery. I edge most of my appliques with blanket stitches.

CUTTING BIAS STRIPS

Fold fabric diagonally with crosswise grain parallel to lengthwise grain; diagonal line of fold is true bias. From this line, measure and mark off strips in parallel lines. (For ginger cookie apron, strips are 2'' wide.) Cut strips apart.

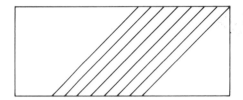

To join strips, lay end of one strip over another, right sides together, so that diagonal seam will be on straight grain of fabric (see sketch). Stitch; press seams open.

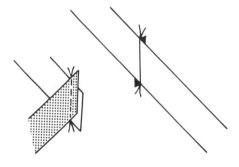

EMBROIDERY STITCHES

Diagrams for embroidery stitches show needle going in and out in one step—this is the clearest way to show you how the stitch is formed. However, you will do most stitches in two steps, pulling needle through to back of fabric, then out again to face of fabric.

Running Stitch. Work right to left, one stitch at a time. Make stitches all same size, with even spaces between stitches.

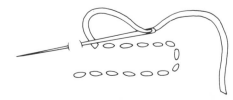

Outline Stitch. Work from left to right; slant stitch slightly across guidelines; keep thread always above needle.

Backstitch. Work from right to left. Bring needle up on guideline; take a stitch to the right; bring needle up again an equal distance ahead; and stitch down again at beginning of last stitch.

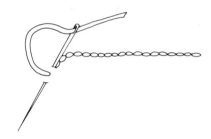

Chain Stitch. Work from top down. Bring needle and thread to front. Make a loop with thread and hold it on fabric with left thumb. Insert needle again, as close as possible to where thread first came up and take a short stitch ahead, drawing needle over loop.

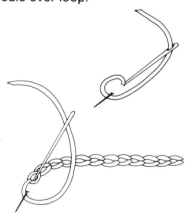

Satin Stitch. Bring needle up on left guideline; insert on right guideline. Carry thread behind work and come up again on first guideline. Keep stitches smooth and close together; each stitch parallel to preceding stitch.

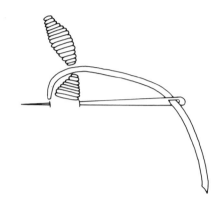

Blanket Stitch. Work left to right (or top to bottom). Imagine two parallel lines. Bring needle out on bottom line; hold thread down with thumb. Insert needle above starting point to the right; bring needle out again on lower line, drawing it over the loop of thread. Pull to make a picket.

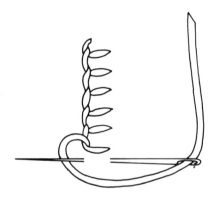

Buttonhole Stitch. Work exactly like blanket stitch but keep stitches close together.

French Knot. Bring needle out where you want embroidered dot. Wrap thread two or three times around point of needle. Insert needle close to spot where thread emerged. Hold knot in place with left thumb and draw thread to wrong side.

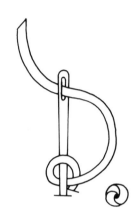